Cat's Tips
to Get the Job
of Your Dreams

by

Catherine Brownlee
Liane Angerman
Karen Cottingham

Authors: Catherine Brownlee, Liane Angerman, Karen Cottingham

Designer: Monika Collins

Available on Amazon.com

ISBN: 9781549932687

As our local and global economy grows and changes, so too must those in the workforce. Those on the job hunt, and even those well established in their careers, must be willing to rethink how they approach employers to ensure they stand out amongst the crowd.

For many years, Catherine Brownlee has been offering her sage advice and helpful feedback to those in the Calgary community and I am so pleased that Catherine, Liane Angerman and Karen Cottingham have put Cat's tips and tricks on paper to be utilized by job seekers around the world.

As we know, the hardest job is often getting a job and *Cat's Tips to Get the Job of your Dreams* offers practical advice that can be applied to any job in any industry. I congratulate Catherine, Liane and Karen for their hard work in putting this book together and I hope all those reading are able to add these tools to your arsenal in finding that dream job.

Naheed K. Nenshi

Mayor of Calgary

TESTIMONIALS

"The combination of Catherine, Liane and Karen's impressive network of contacts in the private industry, government (municipal, provincial and federal) and associations with the tools, expertise and information that are provided in this book present the reader with a platinum toolbox to move forward in their career path. In an ever expanding global economy, this book quickly provides the necessary facts and context to explore job opportunities at a regional, national or international level."

~ Patricia Elliott,
Consul and Senior Trade Commissioner
Canadian Consulate in Los Angeles

"As a business leader, I know there is nothing more important than getting the right people on our teams to do the work that our stakeholders expect of us. *Cat's Tips* will bring outstanding candidates to organizations around the world."

~ Steve Allan,
Chair of Calgary Economic Development
Recipient of the Order of Canada and the Alberta Order of Excellence

"I have seen firsthand the positive influence of Catherine Brownlee's work. Her guidance has made a big difference in the lives of people looking for a new career or expanding their personal networks. I am excited she and her co-authors are now sharing their knowledge and expertise with a global audience."

~ Greg Clark,
MLA for Calgary Elbow

"Having known Catherine for many years, I'm continuously amazed by the art of her matchmaking. Mastering local and international relationships alike, she marries prospective candidates with employers, with the same efficiency as she mediates between a philanthropist and a worthy cause she chooses to support. With a global outlook, for her, it's all about personal relationships; the genuine discourse she applies in all that she touches is the very platform upon which her success is achieved. In *Cat's Tips to Get the Job of our Dreams*, you will learn how you, too, can build these skills for your own success."

~ Dan Levinson,
Co-Founder
Public Safety and Security Research Group

"*Cat's Tips to Get the Job of Your Dreams* gives job-seekers a distinct advantage over their competitors in today's marketplace. With loads of information packed into one easy-to-navigate book, *Cat's Tips* shows you how to write your own success stories, map the career of your dreams and get connected. This book is a timely contribution as we position and re-position ourselves in a shifting economy."

~ Lyn Cadence,
PR Strategist, Publicist and Coach
Cadence PR

"Read chapter two's success stories! Everyone needs to be better at describing what they have accomplished. It makes people interesting as candidates, it helps keep them in their jobs and, let's be realistic, we are all more interesting at a cocktail party if we can describe something we do in an interesting and meaningful way. This is instruction for every aspect of your life."

~ Robynne Anderson,
President
Emerging ag
Canadian Agricultural Hall of Fame Recipient

"Catherine and her team have put together an insightful, actionable guide to landing a job in a world that is evolving faster than it ever has before. This book is a quick read that will surely give you the insights and tools required to not just land any job, but the right job for you. A must-read for those looking to get (and stay) ahead in their job searching efforts."

~ Eric Termuende,
Co-founder NoW Innovations, author of *Rethink Work*

"In a world of ever changing job expectations, with *Cat's Tips to Get the Job of Your Dreams*, Catherine and her team have provided a road map that will take you from where you are now to where you want to go. Every chapter, from 'Do you want the job of your dreams?' to 'Successful Onboarding,' gives you the building blocks to achieve your goal. As with any good map, there are clear and concise directions and you will go back to *Cat's Tips* time and time again."

~ Martin Parnell,
author of *Marathon Quest*, Keynote Speaker, world class endurance athlete five-time Guinness World Record holder and philanthropist

"Meeting Catherine changed my life. I had been on a career break to raise my children and was ready to rejoin the workforce. Looking for work in a tough economic climate is challenging and can be demoralizing but Catherine made me realize you need to look at old problems with new solutions and optimism.

After attending one of Catherine's workshops I was determined to try all the things she and her colleagues had recommended. One of which was saying yes to everything that is legal and moral for the next six months. This was counterintuitive to the way I had always made career decisions. I liked to weigh things up – consider the pros and cons and proceed with caution. However, Catherine was persuasive and her enthusiasm was infectious. I accepted everything that came my way: drinks, receptions, sports events, silent auctions and a wine club.

It was at the last of these where I struck gold. I met a woman who was so interested in my background that she insisted I meet a friend of hers. This friend had been looking to recruit but had not found someone with all the skills she was looking for. The rest, as they say, is history. I had a job within six weeks and I have never looked back."

~ Anna K,
Power Networking class participant

PREFACE

We have been serving and supporting thousands of people on how to get the job of their dreams since 1988. Over the years, we held many seminars that included writing an effective résumé, informational meetings, power networking and successful interviews. During that time, we developed enough content for our 2007 bestseller, *Want to Work in Oil and Gas?* which provided information on how to get employment in the energy industry. Since then, Catherine has been the keynote speaker on these topics at many business-related events and seminars, and is a sessional instructor at local universities. The seminars have been enhanced by the addition of expert Stan Peake, and together they have improved the content to be more impactful and relevant than ever before.

Co-authors, Catherine Brownlee, Liane Angerman and Karen Cottingham, have pulled the new and enhanced content together to ensure you have the tools to land the job of your dreams and reach your highest potential.

Cat's Tips to Get the Job of Your Dreams is written for you who want to learn how to create and execute a plan to attract the job of your dreams ... in any industry ... anywhere in the world.

Contents

CHAPTER ONE

DO YOU WANT THE JOB OF YOUR DREAMS?

"If you can dream it, you can do it."

Walt Disney

INTRODUCTION

In order for you to maximize your career opportunities, it's important for you to understand the professional and business systems in play. Welcome to our world of career empowerment and enhancement. We are about to share with you an assortment of the most helpful tips, resources and tools, which will launch you into the next phase of your own personal career development.

WELCOME TO THE SEARCH WORLD

We recommend a positive relationship with all search firms (not just one) that have the ability to place you into your next job. Recruiters are on the inside track and should be respected for who they know and what they know. Search firms are hired by **clients**[1] who have asked them to find a **candidate**[2] that matches a certain list of criteria. In a slow market, clients can be extremely selective as there are a lot of candidates available who would consider the job. In an up market, however, there are fewer candidates to choose from and clients' criteria may be more relaxed.

If you do not have a relationship with the search firm, it is unlikely they will respond to you unless they have a file that may be of interest to you. Therefore, as a candidate, we recommend sending in your best résumé[3] to all search firms that focus in your area of interest to ensure they have your information and are apprised of what you would consider for a role in the future.

Your preliminary research should include what search firms can offer you. Typically, they are comprised of experts with extensive networks in their areas of specialty. Check out their websites to understand which firms best match your area of interest. Some search firm websites post a comprehensive listing, organized by specialty, industry and contact info. Catherine Brownlee Inc. (CBI) sends out regular newsletters and hosts a networking event regularly.

Provide search agents with your résumé, a cover letter and your business/character references. You may issue a "read receipt" on your email so you can keep track of your efforts. Registration with all firms is important and, once you have sent your information to them, let it go. Not all firms have the capacity to respond to all phone calls and emails. Most agencies will retain quality résumés for future postings.

Once you have connected with a recruiter, send a thank you note within 24 hours of your meeting or conversation. Express your gratitude and willingness to be responsive to their recommendations (ie: career coaching, résumé improvements, appearance, etc.).

Should you be granted an interview with a prospective employer through the search firm, send the interviewer (or hiring manager) a thank you (don't forget to copy the recruiter). Continue to keep the recruiter in the line of communications until (or unless) the content becomes confidential between you and your prospective employer.

Only 10% of your time job seeking should be spent with search firm registration and applying to postings online. The remainder of your time should be invested in **networking** ... everywhere! We have created an entire chapter on this topic: "Networking is the New Black."

[1] **Clients** are organizations that are paying an invoice to the search firm to find them candidates with specific criteria.

[2] **Candidates** do not pay the search firm anything. It is the candidate's responsibility to ensure that his résumé is considered seriously.

[3] **Résumés** may also be referred to as CVs.

NOTES

CHAPTER TWO

PREPPING FOR BREAKTHROUGH

"There is no secret to success: it is the result of preparation, hard work, learning from failure."

General Colin Powell, the Black Collegian

SELF DISCOVERY BEGINS FROM WITHIN

Everything you have achieved to date, in all aspects of your life, is the sum total of what and who you are today. This tally of life's events is an integral factor when you're transitioning your career and considering all of your options.

In her seminars, Catherine enjoys sharing the following analogy of 'repotting.' Understanding the elements required can be extremely valuable and powerful:

Cat's Tool

As a farmer, I visualize a root-bound plant whose growth is stunted by its too-small pot. I know that if it does not get repotted, it will not reach its full growth potential and may even die. Once the plant's roots receive new and fertile soil and have the opportunity to spread in all directions, it is like a rebirth and the plant may now grow to its full potential.

Many of us become complacent and will not likely repot ourselves unless an event threatens our stability or something uncomfortable occurs to motivate the process of change or transition. Quite often fear is the cause of being root-bound. Many people I meet are seeking to transplant themselves to new industries, new countries, new roles and careers. As long as some of the key conditions are met, this can be an ideal platform for new growth to take hold.

Before you begin to repot, you must know what you want. For starters, ask yourself these questions:

- What did you love to do when you were 10 years old?
- What is it that you believe in?
- What do you stand for?
- What gets you jazzed at work?
- What interests you the most?
- What would you try if you knew you could not fail?
- If you could emulate one other person's successes, who would it be?
- What are you willing to do – and not do?
- What can you offer?

Your answers will establish a starting point, and uncover your best place to focus your energies.

Self-discovery starts here! This is the time to assess your skills and interests and all the other factors important to your career. Through your experiences with work, school, hobbies, social activities, volunteer work and leisure activities, you have already developed hundreds of skills and preferences. Now is the time to mine your past and choose the skills, interests and values you want to take forward.

DISCOVERING WHAT YOU WANT

THE LAW OF ATTRACTION

There is a "Law of Attraction" at work here, and it will work for you if you know how to use it. We believe everything that comes into your life you have attracted by virtue of your thoughts and the images you hold or invited in your mind.

Like attracts like, so if you hold onto the thoughts of what you want – let's say working in your area of expertise – those thoughts will help you be in the right place at the right time. Thoughts become actions. Actions become your reality. It really is that simple!

Try imagining yourself already working at the perfect job. Are you in a downtown office or out in a satellite location? Are you with a large or small team? Are you with a commercial organization, a service or manufacturing company? Are you interested in public service or working for a private corporation? What type of work are you doing – sales, administration, accounting, production testing? What types of people surround you – aggressive, assertive, spontaneous, fun, passive, steady? What kind of hours are you working? Thinking about what you want and focusing on it with intention is the first step in making dreams a reality. From here, you must be open to everything that comes your way.

Attract the job, the industry and the people that you want in your life by imagining it all in advance. Keep your dream job top of mind and talk about it as though you already possess it. You will be amazed at what is possible.

This is precisely how you attract possibilities and opportunities to grow, learn and advance.

Cat's Tale

Someone once said when intention comes from a pure place, bearing fruit will be natural. I like to tell a story in our seminars about how my intentions have netted powerful results. My dad was a tool push and, from the time I was a little girl, I always wanted to work for the yellow trucks. When I got older, I learned the company was called FracMaster, one of the world's leading providers of high-pressure oilfield service equipment. Step by step, contact by contact, I did indeed end up working at FracMaster in the sales job of my dreams. Today I am leading CBI, a successful search firm.

It all starts with you!

- Focus on what you want: thoughts become ideas
- Believe in the power of intention
- Be open to possibility: talk about your intentions
- Work hard: actions become realities
- Stay positive

STORYBOOKING YOUR DREAM JOB

Here is one example how Catherine experienced this Law of Attraction first-hand. We recommend you do this too!

Dare to Dream ...

When Catherine was 18, she assembled a storyboard with photos, writings, visual reminders of what she dreamed her future would look like. Some of those items included the following:

- buying a log home with a mountain view

- owning her own business

- travelling to foreign lands

- writing a book

- experiencing great and loving relationships

- always having an open door for those in need

The more tools you use to articulate and visualize the type of job you want, the better able you will be to attract that job into your life.

Cut out images from magazines and books that align with your wants, dreams and desires.

Write down ideas about a perfect day on the job.

Share details with others about what you are looking for.

For free inspiration, check out Barbara Sher's *Wishcraft* online at www.wishcraft.com.

ARTICULATING YOUR POTENTIAL

Your success stories are key!

We are strong advocates of success stories, or Problem/Action/Result Stories (PAR) as they are sometimes called. These success stories are short pieces that capture results you have achieved in the past, and can be applied as quantifiers for future opportunities. Stories need to be specific enough that they can be told with a PAR format. Your stories can be dramatic or ordinary.

WHY DOCUMENT SUCCESS STORIES?

Success stories can:

- Energize us and boost our confidence, particularly when making a career change
- Help us to see our skills and values more clearly
- Point us in the right direction when searching for new opportunities
- Provide employers with evidence of our skills and abilities
- Set us apart from other candidates with similar qualifications
- Help solidify connections
- Help us excel in interview situations

What's important is that you feel proud of these experiences and feel good about your involvement and your accomplishment. These stories are about times when you feel you've made a difference or contributed something of value. We suggest that before connecting with employers you spend time writing out as many stories as you can to refresh your memory and make recall easier.

For each story:

- Start by describing a particular problem (opportunity) or situation you encountered
- Define the action you took
- Explain the results
- Provide a title to each success story, so that you will remember it easily

This may seem an onerous task, but it's time well spent. Once you have your stories documented, you will begin to see patterns of skill sets emerge. Beyond your training, education or work history, these stories provide concrete evidence of your unique value to an employer.

You will use these stories repeatedly when you begin to network. They will help guide you to companies where you can add value and you will include them – in condensed versions – within your cover letters and résumés. And you will not succeed in a behavioural descriptive interview without a story lineup, proving you have the skills you say you have.

GET SPECIFIC

Remember, your stories need to be specific enough they can be told inside of a few minutes applying the PAR format.

We recommend you scale down your story to a more specific incident or series of incidents. "Working in Engineering," for example, is not a story in and of itself. Rather, it involves hundreds of specific stories where you project managed, trouble shot, coached, mentored, assisted, solved problems, etc.

GET STARTED

Don't know where to start? Your stories can be found in the following:

- Situations when you turned a negative into a positive
- Things that you built, fixed or improved
- Projects that you implemented, participated in or completed
- Procedures that you developed or used to save time or headaches
- Risks that you took in order to undertake new challenges
- Your travel, volunteer work, community work, course work, hobbies
- New skills or key learnings you initiated through work or key leisure pursuits
- Times when you resolved conflict between colleagues, peers or clients
- Times when you helped someone else with a problem or challenge
- Ideas you had for improving the way things were done

You may surprise yourself with how many stories you have.

Always create a title for your PAR story.

Now that you have established directives by learning and exercising the laws of attraction and documented your PAR stories, you are now ready to put yourself out there and use these new tools to ascertain your next best career role. This next section will help you sort out where best to apply your efforts and achieve the results your dream and deserve.

PLANNING YOUR PATHWAY

Throughout one's career, the criteria for your ideal role will continually shift. Before you even apply for a position, you must do some prep work, like determining the criteria for your career move. These are critical questions, which will most definitely influence your job search.

Money is always a major consideration.

Lifestyle is also a major consideration influencing your employment selection and options.

Here is a handy tool that can help you sort your priorities and focus your efforts into the actions required to meet your current objectives:

Criteria	Description
Responsibilities	What responsibilities in my next role will advance my career plan/path? Does this position align my long- and short-term goals (career-wise, financial, personal, etc.)? Am I qualified to undertake this role?
Location	Does the location of the role fit my lifestyle? Is relocation an option? Would I be willing/able to accept a transfer or relocate myself, my family, or commute effectively?
Compensation	What is an acceptable range of remuneration? Am I willing to job share? Would I be willing to accept a lower salary during a downturn? Is there room for growth? Bonus structure?

Benefits	What benefits are important to me at this stage in life? Am I willing to exercise flexibility in the types of benefits offered by an organization?
Vacation	What lifestyle and vacation patterns should I consider prior to negotiating a final contract?
Transportation and Parking	What are all the transportation options (parking, bus, train, etc.?). Is there compensation for any of these? What is the transit time and potential restrictions from my place of residence should weather or traffic become a factor?
Stock Options or Bonus Structure	What are the pros and cons?

CAREER MAPPING

Our friend and past colleague, Carmen Goss, is a great career coach. Carmen has provided us with the material for this section.

The first step after your visualization exercise is to build out the following steps:

Career Map Step	Action
Start at Start	List what you are currently making and take an honest look at where you are professionally right now.
Identify your strengths	Capture the three key strengths that you are the "go to person" for. Ask your boss, co-workers and best friends to help you identify your key strengths. These strengths must be unique to you!
List the conditions you want in your professional life	Work, environment, culture, leadership, levels of responsibility, hours worked, commute and/or location, flexibility, vacation, benefits.
Capture what success means to YOU	How much money would you like to make and what kinds of things will you be doing to earn this money? Your visualization exercise is very helpful in capturing success

Identify your purpose	What were you put on this planet to do professionally? Once you know why you are here, you will figure out what you need to do next. Getting this captured well may take the assistance of a Career Coach. It is worth it and so are you!
Go and get it!	Now that you know where you are going, you can create the steps and take the action required to make it happen. You can customize your résumé, network effectively in the right industries, apply for the roles you truly desire, interview well, and negotiate a great offer!

LIFE BALANCE

Our colleague, Stan Peake, of InSite Performance Coaching, says,

"Anyone who tells you that they have 'life balance' figured out, or that they have a foolproof system, is just kidding themselves.

Life balance means that each area of life that truly matters to you becomes a priority, but you can't do it all at once. While you are taking care of your body getting an early workout in, you are sacrificing sleep. While you are busy networking to build the business, you are missing your daughter's piano recital. While you are taking your son to hockey, you are missing a phone call from a customer, and while you prioritize your relationship and go for a date night, you are missing beers with the guys.

Life balance is about sacrifice. What are you willing to sacrifice today and regularly for the next few years in order to have success in these selected areas of your life? If you want to be above average, you are going to have to sacrifice some fun now for delayed payoffs as a result of your hard work. You can have it all, but not all of the time, every day. Life balance, then, is about balancing your sacrifices."

CHAPTER THREE

RÉSUMÉS AND LETTERS THAT GET READ

"The challenge of life, I have found, is to build a résumé that doesn't simply tell a story about what you want to be, it's a story about who you want to be."

Oprah Winfrey

How vital is a good résumé? Your résumé is your introduction (or calling card). Search experts throughout the world will emphasize the immense value of owning a résumé that is well written, up-to-date and industry-appropriate. This chapter will reveal the essentials of the best résumés and illustrate the difference between good résumés and the ones that secure the job. At the end of the chapter, we will walk through the essentials of creating and presenting your skills with effective letters:

- Cover Letter
- Request for Info Meeting Letter
- Proposal Letter
- Follow-Up Letter
- Thank You Letter

Cat's Tip

If you don't have an extensive work history yet (ie: students), start with your achievements in education and volunteering.

Writing your own résumé is one of the most difficult tasks any of us will do when looking for a position: **hire an expert to do an expert job.**

DESIGN PRINCIPLES

The design of your résumé is as important as its content. Many recruiters will tell you that they have probably missed good candidates because the résumé was too difficult to read, or did not emphasize the qualities or skills required.

There are two things to remember: **keep the look clean, and don't be afraid of white space.**

FORMATS

Reverse Chronological

- Key feature is stating your most current job first and listing your timelines backwards from there
- This format is most effective when your career has followed a meaningful path within one profession or graduated role (ie: a dancer who began her career as a teacher's studio helper then

advanced to play a lead role in a stage performance, to becoming an agent for the dance company and later owning the agency)

- This format is often used when you want to progress to the next higher level within your profession or industry of choice

Functional

- This format is skills-focused and typically contains several categories that showcase specific areas you have mastered or gained valuable insights in
- Used when you are transitioning from one type of profession into another or new one
- Applied if you are trying to grow new skills and already have some experience
- Can be used to draw attention to areas that may not be evident or obvious
- May also be used when you wish to remove the attention from your chronology (ie: you've worked in a broad spectrum of industries, or have job hopped, both of which can be detrimental to the reader's first impression of you)

Hybrids

- Hybrids are combinations of various formats that work for your needs and are formulated by how best to showcase your uniqueness and convey the cleanest presentation
- Résumé professionals will often use a hybrid when working with a client whose career contains sensitive issues (such as periods of unemployment or illness), or unique skill sets that don't apply to the majority of the roles they've held
- Hybrids showcase content that appeals to the needs of both the applicant and the vacancy; it accentuates pertinent experience gained within one or more roles (and usually are required to qualify for an opportunity)

Cat's Tip

TEXT FORMATTING

It's not difficult to create a reader-friendly résumé that is visually appealing. Ensure a consistent style throughout the entire document: titles, font size, bullets, tabs, numbering, spacing and so on.

Keep the text formatting simple to make it easy to read. When too much is emphasized, nothing stands out. Try to keep the amount of italics and underlines to a minimum. The human eye identifies words by their shape more than by the letters.

Cat's Tip

There is selective value in using all caps, such as your name or title role and even effectively applied to category headings. Both help create importance and flow to the résumé.

Apply caution when using ALL CAPS as this makes each word the same rectangular shape, thus making it harder to read quickly. Research shows that words in all caps take far longer to comprehend, bogging down your résumé, and can imply screaming.

FONT

Avoid less common fonts, even if they seem more interesting. If your résumé is sent electronically or being scanned, you can't be sure that your readers' systems contain non-standard fonts. If they do not, your font will be substituted for another, which may negatively impact all your careful spacing and formatting. Better to appear a bit boring and clean than exciting and difficult to read. To avoid shifts in formatting, **always make a PDF of your résumé** prior to emailing it.

Depending on the font you use, the font size should be 11 pt or 12 pt. Choose a font that is common to most platforms and easy to read. There are two major subdivisions in font type: serif and sans serif. Serif fonts are considered easier to read. We recommend Tahoma (sans serif), Calibri (sans serif) and Garamond (serif).

LETTERHEAD

It is important to create a letterhead that will be transferred to the top of all your job search correspondence, such as your résumés, letters, projects and reference lists.

Your letterhead will identify your name – big and bold to show healthy ego – followed by your telephone and email coordinates in slightly smaller font. Letterhead can be left- or right-justified, or centered at the top of the page. Only include coordinates where you want to receive communications regarding your job search. Be sure to use the phone number that you and only you are responsible to answer. Use a personal, yet professional voicemail message and email address.

While you can certainly include your city of residence as part of your letterhead, it's not necessary to give your complete mailing address, and given privacy and safety concerns, we do not recommend it. Some people choose to state their address on their résumé as a status achievement, but sometimes this works against them when competing for a position.

The pages following your résumé's first page should contain a header and/or a footer, which includes, at minimum, your full name on the left and the page number on the right.

Never include a picture or personal information such as date of birth, marital status or government identification numbers.

BULLETS

Bulleted lists on résumés are much loved by recruiters, because they serve to:

- Increase readability and flow
- Make your information easier to understand and find
- Make it possible to use a lead-in phrase, thus avoiding repetition
- Make your accomplishments stand out

In the list above, each bullet starts with a capital letter and uses no punctuation at the end. You can choose whatever format you like for your résumé as long as you are consistent. Remember, less is often more and white space on a résumé serves much value.

Cat's Tip

Avoid listing 'soft skills,' (such as "hard-working" or "team player") because everyone subscribes to these types of skills at some juncture. Give the recruiter something more. Attach specific relevance to the position you are vying for:

- Achieved top sales, five years running
- Consistently exceeded quotas
- Promoted three times in five years

SENDING YOUR RÉSUMÉ ELECTRONICALLY

Companies will request a certain format to apply or send your résumé to them online. Follow their instructions carefully and answer or address all of their requests. If you avoid filling in some fields, when the competition is fierce and there are many candidates to choose from, you may be overlooked because of this omission.

CHOOSING A GREAT EMAIL SUBJECT HEADING

When you email an introduction letter, remember that if the receiver doesn't recognize your name, your letter could be deleted before it's ever read.

The following are examples to make sure your email is opened:

- State the name of the person referring you in the subject heading: "referred by John Dunsworth, ABC Energy Company."

- Research the person you're sending the letter to and add something pertinent to them in the subject heading. For example, one candidate found out that the man she wanted to meet had climbed Mount Kilimanjaro to raise money for cancer research. She used the subject heading: "Kilimanjaro in the office."

RÉSUMÉ CONTENT ... PUTTING IT ALL TOGETHER

Résumé trends have changed, particularly if you are applying during a busy market cycle. Résumés must always be polished, accurate and readable. Gone are the days of résumé styles which are much too dense and text heavy. The reason is simple: consider a day in the life of Catherine's recruiting firm, where they receive an average of 300 résumés each day. Résumés with lots of white space and clear, short bullets of information can be quickly scanned to determine their match with current and upcoming opportunities. It's a win-win for recruiters and candidates alike.

Professional résumé writer and co-author of this book, Liane Angerman, recommends the following categories (or features) for most résumé formats:

1. A clearly stated Objective.

2. Career Summary or Highlighted Qualifications, presented as a summary statement followed by a bulleted list of accomplishments, quantified with dollars, percentages, and measured results when possible.

3. Career or Professional Experience*, including job titles, company names and dates of employment, listed in reverse

chronological order. Bullet points will be included underneath the jobs of most relevance.

4. Education and Professional Development*, including a listing of degrees, diplomas and certificates, job tickets as well as relevant courses and seminars.

5. Community/Volunteer Activity.

6. Computer Experience (or "Added Value"), including your proficiency with a range of software programs, or specific qualifications that bolster your fit for the position you're applying for.

7. Additional relevant highlights such as Professional Affiliations and Activities, Accomplishments, Accreditations or Awards, Hobbies and Other Interests, and Publications.

*Note: switch order of 3 and 4 above, depending on which is most recent or pronounced.

Let's explore these features individually.

PART 1: STATE YOUR OBJECTIVE

Stating an Objective at the top of your résumé is a wise strategy for everyone, particularly for those transitioning from one industry to another. Your Objective should indicate that you know what you want, who you are, express your expertise and guide the reader towards your upcoming ideal role.

The Objective should be customized for every job you apply for. If you are responding to an advertised position, the Objective is the job title itself. Otherwise, your Objective should be specific and conveyed in only one or two brief sentences.

Your Objective will include three elements:

• The job you want to be considered for

• What you bring to the position

• What you want from your future employer

Here's an example of an Objective statement that helped a candidate secure a position:

> "A technical sales expert who values high-touch client service, and is searching for an organization that believes in professional development and industry advancement."

PART 2: CAREER SUMMARY OR HIGHLIGHTED QUALIFICATIONS

Start by providing a statement of your years of experience and areas of expertise. Be sure to include any relevant experience you have had, even if it was 20 years ago.

> "Over 20 years of progressively responsible experience in sales and marketing in the transportation and utility industry, culminating in promotion to regional manager."

Next, add a few bulleted points giving evidence of your skills; it is your best achievements in summary form:

- Consistently exceeded quotas
- Consistently received excellent ratings from participants
- Promoted three times within five years
- Promoted from shipper/receiver to production manager over a 10-year career span

The Career Summary section is where it is important to show measured results wherever possible. Numbers and percentages are easy to read and reveal your successes instantly.

This is often the first section recruiters read and you may lose them if you do not use terminology applicable to their team or needs.

You can captivate your reader by knowing what they need through research and a peppering of industry words throughout your documents (cover letter and résumé). Decision makers get a sense that the candidate already has her finger on the pulse of the industry, speaks the language, carries confidence and is likely a match for the position. This tactic is called echoing the reader and allows you to fit your message to specific needs.

Recognitions such as "Volunteer of the Year" or "Woman of Distinction" would go here as well. If you received a bonus every year because of performance, this is where you can include this detail.

Include a particularly glowing sentence from a performance review. For example,

> Manager wrote on performance review that, "Tom's powerful vision and team leading skills catapulted the team to the highest rank in the country."

A personal touch can also be added here. For example, an administrative assistant included the phrase "Known as the ray of sunshine in the office" in her career summary and was offered an interview with each résumé she sent out.

Your highlights are 'wow' moments you own and can speak proudly of at the interview.

This category is a great place to showcase your top achievements: GPA, testimonials from clients or colleagues, awards, etc. Recruiters read this section and gauge the value, language and credibility of a potential candidate by their chosen words and accomplishments.

- Include awards received for exemplary results, or special training
- Sales volumes met or surpassed consecutively, or in challenging markets
- Volumes of products, numbers of clients, measured results of areas served, etc.
- Names of major clients, countries you've worked in, credentials you've achieved
- List no more than five or six and keep them in bullet format

Example:

> - Saved employer $250k (over three years) in upgrades through sound analysis and increased performance by 65%, decreased costs by 20%

- Developed a high availability solution for a master data management system, involving 3-node rac cluster
- Performed complete lifecycle of new Oracle security system at hospital, to include 380 staff members, inside first six months, exceeding employer's expectation
- Diversified technology across broad spectrum of clients and industries across globe
- Led multi-disciplinary tech team of 35 people for $20m multi-stage, project expanded five times and increased revenues by 33% over five years
- Succeeded full completion of building, producing and testing>50 databases, etc.

Cat's Tip

When stating your accomplishment (in verb form), use past tense only.

To avoid confusion and mix-ups of tense, write every point as though it happened in the past – even if you are currently serving in a position.

Change "Managing" to "Managed," etc.

Compare the following two examples for the bulleted points of the Career Summary:

Candidate One	Candidate Two
Career Summary	**Career Summary**
Strong sales and marketing skills	Managed sales and marketing **portfolios of $1.5M plus** in the IT, real estate, pharmaceutical and energy sectors
Excellent management skills	
Skilled at building relationships	
Demonstrated ability to build teams	**Managed a core team of 12** specialized engineering and technical functions and advised executive management committees on overall strategy
Strong financial management	

	Developed key strategic alliances and **managed approximately 50 supplier/vendor relationships** with partners and competitors, including abc, xxx, yyy
	Coordinated professional, technical, support and management teams to meet the challenges of reorganization and high growth business development

If you were the recruiter and had only the above section of the résumé to go on, which candidate would you have a better sense of? Which candidate would you choose to meet first? Candidate Two, of course!

Here is another career summary example that helped land this client her job:

High energy, creative and versatile executive with 11 years cross-functional success in leadership, marketing/community relations, project management and team development. Knack for relationship marketing, media relations and employee morale. Strong performance in market share and revenue/ROI growth.

- Progressively promoted to director level as a result of consistently exceeding financial goals and exhibiting strong team-building and leadership abilities

- Successfully designed and implemented market development strategies resulting in 15% year-on-year growth

- Proven history of successfully managing multiple projects simultaneously, resulting in financial expectations with all event goals met or exceeded

- Coordinated and implemented national sponsorship partnerships resulting in 25% increased revenues for involved projects

- All direct reports have won company awards, such as Sales Leadership, Customer Service, Manager of the Year and Salesperson of the Year

"Anne is a focused, motivated manager who sets high standards and achieves her goals."

"First Four Inches" Rule

I can't stress enough how important the first half page of your résumé is! Recruiters open your résumé to see if you have anything applicable for the positions they currently have available. Most have neither the time nor the patience to scroll through page after page to find out if your skills and experience are applicable or not.

Your résumé must convince recruiters in those first four inches, or you've likely lost your chance.

EXPERTISE

Simply put, this next section of your résumé summarizes what you are good at. And we don't mean motherhood statements like "hard worker" or "good attention to detail."

This section is particularly important if you are making a career change or if some of your best highlights were in jobs held years ago. **The purpose is to make a case that your achievements and career are directly relevant to the position you are applying for.**

You can give this section any number of titles including Career Summary, Highlights of Qualifications, Areas of Expertise, Professional Achievements, or Career Synopsis to name a few.

Are you a sales and marketing professional? If so, outline your expertise in market research, identifying client needs and developing sales solutions.

Do you have experience in leading teams? Then state that by mentioning how large the team was and other important information.

Experience in managing budgets? Then indicate the size of budget you have managed; illustrate the numbers you were responsible for when you started, what the deliverables were and how these have increased over time.

Additional training or special skills? If you have a Masters degree or Ph. D, add the title to your name at the top of the résumé. However, if you have special training like project management, production accounting or leadership from the London School of Business and it is applicable to what you're applying for, add it here. If you had a great GPA, add it here as well.

PART 3: CAREER EXPERIENCE (OR PROFESSIONAL EXPERIENCE)

Now you can talk about what you've been doing all these years, in reverse chronological order.

It is important to include the details of what you have been doing throughout your entire career. Account for each year since you completed your education. **Any gaps may lead the recruiter to assume you are trying to hide something.** There is nothing wrong with stating you were on maternity leave or caring for a sick parent. If you travelled the world, indicate the countries you visited. Present yourself openly from the very beginning. This type of energy and honesty will help you attract the right position and the right company.

Show everything – even summer work and volunteer experiences. Decision makers might know people in the companies where you have worked, and this is precisely what may help get your foot in the door.

LAYOUT

The layout of your text is important. When introducing your career experience section, consider this sequencing and layout:

Big Company, Tel Aviv, Israel   1990 to present
Information Technology Project Manager

Here are a few extra tips for laying out your career experience:

If you were promoted several times inside the same company, you need only state the name of the company and the total years worked once. Make it look like one natural progression.

If the reader is unlikely to recognize your former employer or type of company from its name, describe the nature of the business briefly in a bracketed phrase underneath the company name.

Add more bulleted points under the jobs most applicable to the position you are applying for (five bullets maximum). Expand by showing measured results with numbers and percentages.

Remember, it is your job to take the reader's work out of interpreting your résumé.

Cat's Tip

Ageism is only a factor if you allow it to be

Embrace your age and experience and go all the way back on your résumé. With the worldwide labour shortage, as well as the lack of skilled and professional workers in all disciplines, employers have started welcoming candidates with more experience.

Mature workers with vast knowledge and experience will be preferred for a number of positions – especially in leadership roles.

PART 4: EDUCATION AND PROFESSIONAL DEVELOPMENT

Education includes a listing of degrees, diplomas and certificates that come with credentials (ie: B.A. Arts). Professional development includes a listing of courses and seminars. If you are a professional requiring numerous courses annually and have pages of ongoing development, put the most notable courses under the professional development heading and then include a full list as a separate document. Be sure to include where you studied and the year you graduated, particularly in the education section. (Note: recent graduates typically list education before their career experience.)

Example:

FORMAL EDUCATION AND PROFESSIONAL DEVELOPMENT:

Essential Management Skills for Emerging Leaders (Division of Continuing Ed., Professional Development)	Harvard University, Cambridge, MA	2017
Petroleum Engineering Technology Certification	SAIT, Calgary, AB	2001
Chemical Engineering (Natural Gas Processing)	University of Calgary	2000
Professional Engineering Certification (P. Eng)		1996
B. Sc in Mechanical Engineering	University of Saskatchewan	1994

ADDITIONAL COURSES:

- Modern Well Test Analysis
- Evaluation of Canadian Oil & Gas Properties (Sproule)
- Production Operations (OGCI)
- Open Hole Log Evaluation (Schlumberger)
- Tickets: H2s Alive, Whmis, TDG

PART 5: COMMUNITY OR VOLUNTEER ACTIVITY

Because more and more recruiters are looking for community or volunteer activity, everything in this area is critical. Many places in the world are known to be highly philanthropic. It's important to point to where your volunteer experience has been focused. This should include any board of directors experience, such as a member, a chairman, etc. Even your volunteer church or school commitments can be added. By letting your personality shine through, you will be better positioned to make valuable connections, attract the right opportunity and align with a suitable corporate culture.

When formatting this section, use the same structure as you used for your career experience section.

For example:

PHILANTHROPY AND LEISURE INTERESTS:
- Coaching minor sports teams including hockey and lacrosse
- Camping and hiking
- Executive treasurer for community association of seniors, raised $15k via sponsors

If there were measurable results, be sure to include those too.

PART 6: COMPUTER EXPERIENCE

It's important to point out your proficiency with software programs. This becomes absolutely essential for scanned résumés. If recruiters or employers are looking for a specific skill, program or software experience not listed on your résumé, you might lose your opportunity at the scanning stage.

Whether you are an executive or frontline worker, list software expertise such as Outlook, Word, PowerPoint, any database management software, etc. If you have experience working with a customized system, list the software program's title, followed by a brief explanation in brackets. Differentiate your experience according to "Proficient in," and "Working Knowledge of."

PROGRAMS AND SOFTWARE:

- OMS SuperUser
- SAP (auditing)
- Microsoft Suite
- AccuMap
- GeoStat

PART 7: PROFESSIONAL AFFILIATIONS AND ACTIVITIES

Include the professional association you belong to and how long you have been a member. You may also include past memberships. If you have served on any committees or task forces, display the description of your activities in the same way you portrayed your job descriptions in the Career Experience section. Example:

Director	Edmonton Association of Continuing Education and Recreation, 2004
	Not-for-profit organization distributes ~$12m in provincial educational funding annually
Member	Association of Professional Engineers and Geoscientists of Alberta (APEGA)

If you find your association listing is too large, shave off the ones that are no longer applicable to where you want to be next. We suggest that you do include as many as you can; there's a chance the hirer knows of the association and may be passionate about it, which will increase your chances of being granted an interview. Listing religious associations is appropriate and can be listed in a discretionary manner.

PART 8: ACCOMPLISHMENTS, ACCREDITATIONS OR AWARDS

This section may actually include accomplishments that you would not normally think important. They are your "moments of glory" and can bring to light your drive and determination – qualities important to the majority of employers. Winning a gold medal in the small garden category of the horticultural society garden contest might be precisely what sets you apart from otherwise similar candidates.

If you are unsure which awards, achievements or accomplishments should be included, be sure to get a second opinion.

PART 9: HOBBIES AND OTHER INTERESTS

Why are hobbies and other interests important for your next role? Again, this is another way to set you apart and show who you really are. Everything counts. If you play hockey, for instance, put it down – especially if you are a goalie. You might get called just because the company needs an extra player at Friday's league game. If you are a golfer, mention this. Common interests and hobbies are a great way to connect with those doing the hiring and fit in with the existing culture of a company. It also shows you have a life outside of work and can balance the demands of both work and life.

PART 10: PUBLICATIONS

If you have been published, list those publications that relate directly to your career goal. Employers most interested in publications will be research organizations, consulting, and international organizations. If you have a long list of publications, we recommend you create a separate list, using your letterhead at the top of the page.

SUE LI   **Organizational Strategist**

Email: sue.li@gmail.com
Social media links here
+2.783.555.5555
London, England

OBJECTIVE

To contribute strong business analysis and development skills in a management capacity within a dynamic, high-growth organization.

CAREER SUMMARY

An achievement-oriented manager experienced at developing effective program strategies that meet both customer and organizational goals. Highlights include:

- Implementation of an agile approach to delivering projects at GreatCom

- Recipient of a GreatCom National Innovation Award for completing a complex, $2.2M project on time, within scope and a budget balanced to $600

- Driving and leading a product transformation activity for Integration Group that led to increased sales average over three years of 87%

- Obtained Personal Leadership Certificate from Royal Roads University

PROFESSIONAL EXPERIENCE

GreatCom, London, England   **2000 – 2006**

Portfolio Manager, Reporting to the Vice President IT

A senior project manager, accountable for the total "health" of a portfolio representing a group of related projects. Responsible for GreatCom's integrated execution strategy and acted as the primary interface between portfolio leaders, governance Committee and project teams. Performed a liaison role to ensure the programs and projects delivered to strategic business priorities.

- Successfully implemented an agile delivery and iterative development approach to project management to drive low-cost product growth in a rapid delivery environment resulting in a 35% reduction in costs

- Managed several complex projects including a national new technology initiative with a cost of $2.2M that was delivered on time, within scope and to a budget balanced to within $600
- Project managed the IT component for audit compliance, eliminated 26 areas of non-compliance
- Managed the day-to-day contract implementation

Acting Manager, Corporate PMO   2000 – 2003

Responsible for directing and managing all cross-functional corporate projects that touched GreatCom's internal customers. Provider of strong leadership to ensure all projects successfully designed and maintained in a way that met the needs of GreatCom and its customers.

- Developed and implemented a new business assessment and project development process that aligned project delivery framework across divisions
- Led a team of nine with careful attention paid to GreatCom's leadership attributes while meeting stakeholder expectations and balancing competing demands
- Reduced attrition to zero by conducting quarterly team building, mentoring and coaching sessions to accelerate team development for high performance and to inspire extraordinary results

Integration Group, Vancouver, BC   1996 – 2000

Reporting to the Vice President and Chief Information Officer

Responsible for identifying opportunities for business process improvements and technology solutions that achieved business goals by working closely with customers, vendors and senior management to ensure projects were managed on budget and on schedule.

- Co-managed the assessment, procurement and implementation of a $400k national transportation system project that was delivered on budget, on time and within scope
- Served as internal business consultant by working closely with various functional groups in assessing, developing and executing projects relating to their departments
- Developed key strategic alliances and managed approximately 50 supplier/vendor relationships with partners and competitors
- Conducted market studies in several international markets for new product lines
- Developed a project prioritization, ranking and governance model to ensure that the right projects were executed to meet integration group's short- and medium-term strategic objectives

Western Communications, Vancouver, BC 1990 – 1995

Project Manager/Business Analyst, Reporting to the Associate Director of Information Services

Responsible for contributing to the objectives of the information services department by coordinating, monitoring and directing customer and technical requests, ensuring appropriate action taken in resolving client issues, assisting senior management in operational issues, and acting as liaison between various technical and user groups.

- Supported external consultants by providing issue identification, system clarification and data gathering in order to integrate three marketing systems

EDUCATION

Bachelor of Arts in Economics, London School of Business, 1987

PROFESSIONAL DEVELOPMENT
In progress – Project Management Professional (PMP)

VOLUNTEERING
Canyon Meadows Community Association

BOARD POSITIONS
Canadian Diabetes Association Canvasser

Canadian Cancer Society Canvasser

COMPUTER SKILLS
Proficient with:

- MS Word, MS Excel, MS Access, MS Project, MS Power Point
- PEAK (data management software)

Working knowledge of:

- Frontpage

REFERENCES

It is always a good idea to include references along with your résumé – especially character references. Including your references shows who you know and who is willing to vouch for you. If the recruiter knows one or more of your contacts, they will feel more comfortable taking the next step in your application.

A strong reference must:
- Consent (in advance)
- Be available to accept reference requests

- Want you to succeed
- Be able to articulate your strengths

References have additional influence if they know the industry and/or the company and its players.

Character References

Your references should be a separate document with the same letterhead you created for your cover letter and résumé. Always ask references in advance before including their names on your list. Likewise, obtain appropriate phone numbers and/or email addresses to list as contact information. Home phone numbers should never be given (unless granted by your reference for this use), and formal mailing addresses are not necessary (email will suffice). Be sure to ask your reference what they would say when they are asked "what is the candidate's greatest weakness?" You might want to sit down with a few of your references and share the kinds of questions they could potentially be asked by recruiters. Preparing for a reference check is a good idea, particularly if it has been a few years since you have worked together.

Here is a list of the questions CBI asks all referees:

- **Position Held/Work Performed:** what type of work did the person do for your company?

- **Strengths and Technical Abilities:** how would you rate the person's technical knowledge as it related to the position? Did the person know what was required and did he/she learn inside of a reasonable time frame?

- **Flexibility:** in terms of scheduling, adapting to change, etc. Have you encountered any problems with this person in these areas? If yes, please elaborate on the situation.

- **Pace and Deadlines:** please comment on the person's effectiveness performing in a highly dynamic environment. Describe to me what "dynamic" is; that is, give me some words around what fast-paced looks like.

- **Organizational and Time Management Skills:** please comment on the person's ability to plan, organize, and prioritize work, especially in multi-task situations.

- **Interpersonal Skills:** please comment on this person's ability to relate to and communicate with people. What do/did others in your company like most about this person?

- **Problem Solving and Learning:** how would you evaluate the person's ability to grasp concepts, learn new things, question, solve problems and analyze information, etc?

- **Trustworthiness/Reliability:** please comment in areas of trustworthiness, dependability and reliability, etc.

- **Conflict Resolution:** have you ever seen this person in a situation of conflict or heated emotions? If you have, please unfold the situation for me. How did the person behave? Was the person's behaviour effective? What was the end result?

- **Area for Improvement:** we all have them. In what area(s) do you feel this person should improve? What steps has this person taken in terms of self-improvement?

- **Reason for Departure:** would you happen to know why this person is considering leaving his/her current position or why this person left the position when you worked together?

- **Candidate for Rehire/Continued Association:** given an opportunity, would you rehire or work with this person again? If so, in what capacity?

- **Additional Information:** is there anything I have not asked, but that I should be aware of that would help us with the decision to hire?

It's fair for you to know in advance the kinds of things your references will say about you during a reference check. Whatever you can do to jog their memories and help them remember detailed information about you and your work will serve to your advantage. Likewise, the more they know about the positions you are applying for, the better.

This is particularly important if you feel there may be a negative reference response on your list. By discussing potential questions and responses in advance, you will be able to grow from the opportunity to learn the good and not-so-good about how you performed your job responsibilities. And if required, you can remove some references from your list and choose others instead.

As with business references, your character reference section should include their full name, title, company and appropriate coordinates.

BUSINESS REFERENCES

Business references include people you have worked with.

Have no fewer than three and no more than five business references. If possible, include at least one past or current supervisor, one past or current co-worker and, if you have been a manager, at least one past subordinate or mentee. If you have not been a manager, include a second past supervisor or co-worker.

Include your reference's full name, business title, current company, and contact coordinates, including work telephone and email. Also include a short phrase outlining the relationship that you had with that person, as well as the name of the company you worked at during the time of your business association.

Here is how your reference information can be formatted:

> Catherine Shelby, President
> Great Big Oil Company
> Telephone: 403 555 1212
> Email: c.shelby@gbo.com
> Former supervisor at Shell Canada

CHARACTER REFERENCES

Who should be on your list?

If you do not have enough experience in a certain area, a character reference may be the person who gets you the initial interview. It is all about "who you know." Therefore, including character references of people already in the industry you are applying to would be beneficial. Who should be on your list? Include all your contacts who know you well enough to comment on whether you would fit inside a particular company. The bigger the list you can provide the better, even if it covers two full pages. If you can show that you have a large network, and recruiters and decision makers happen to know at least one or more of your references, they will likely phone those with whom they have connections.

As their reputation is at stake, character references will be very honest as to whether or not they see you as a fit in a particular company. This makes their opinions particularly valued.

As with business references, your character reference section should include their full name, title, company and appropriate coordinates.

COVER LETTERS

Ah, the dreaded cover letter. Many people are afraid of writing this document. However, once you understand its purpose, and have an outline in hand, it becomes more a matter of filling in the blanks appropriately than of penning the next great prose. You want to ensure anything important from your résumé is also captured briefly in your cover letter.

While the majority of cover letters are not read, it is still a required document today for most applications. However, we predict they will be eliminated in the future. In the meantime, you will want to ensure that anything important from your résumé is also captured briefly in your cover letter and email.

Many on-line applications demand that you attach the cover letter directly to your résumé (all within the same document). **Read the directions carefully, since you may be excluded from the opportunity if you cannot follow simple directions.** Always, always add one.

COVER LETTER TO A SEARCH FIRM

This letter accompanies your résumé and tells the search firm the kinds of positions you are applying to. This covering letter acts as an introduction and a statement of intent for the overall communication.

The cover letter is often ignored by recruiters. Nonetheless, you must not skip this step. While your cover letter must be as compelling as you can make it, be sure that your résumé is complete in itself, including all the information you want the recruiter to see. The résumé is the document that will definitely be read.

Example:

YOUR LETTERHEAD HERE
(same as your résumé)

Date

Company and Address

Attention: Name and Title

Dear Mr. Smithers,

RE: Upcoming Opportunities for Success

I am amazed at how XYZ Company helps organizations define, build, measure, and expand their Internet strategy and presence. XYZ has a legacy of creating effective and distinctive interactive solutions for some of the most admired companies in the world. Additionally, I am impressed that Forrester Research has recognized you with the highest score for its current offering for the second year in a row. This is most inspiring and makes XYZ very appealing to me.

It is my understanding that there may be some exciting opportunities at XYZ that are in keeping with my current goals, and it is with great enthusiasm that I am sending you my résumé for consideration.

My experience and achievements, which are detailed in the enclosed résumé, include:

- Six years of management responsibilities with GreatCom's PMO
- Implementation of an agile method of delivering

projects with focus on delivering superior business value by accelerating project delivery, reducing costs and increasing quality through application of several rapid delivery practices

- Personal Leadership Certificate from Royal Roads University

- Recipient of a GreatCom national innovation award for completing a complex, $2.2m project on time, within scope and to a budget balanced to within $600

- Thirteen years of experience in marketing/sales and project management in the telecommunications industry

- Track record of developing creative strategic solutions with diverse partners in dynamic domestic and international marketing relationships

I understand the big picture as well as the bottom line and take great pride in a job well done. I am flexible and able to move between roles while handling multiple tasks.

I look forward to speaking with you about XYZ opportunities and will follow-up this communication within the next few business days.

Best regards,

Your Name

Enc. Résumé and references

Cat's Tip

Avoid the use of antiquated jargon, such as "Dear Sir or Madam" or "To whom it may concern." Do your best to obtain a name and title, and if your efforts fail, address the letter to the company and use a Subject or Attention line (or both) instead of a salutation. Unless you know of a good reason not to, always address women as Ms. instead of Mrs. or Miss. Circumstances can change in a blink and you don't want to use the wrong title.

COVER LETTER WHEN RESPONDING TO AN AD

This letter tells the person reading your correspondence the purpose of your writing. Your cover letter, if compelling, can help land your résumé into the keeper versus reject pile.

When responding to an ad, it's important to identify the specific position you are applying for. You can certainly use a subject line that includes the job posting number and where it was posted before you launch into the letter itself. Write down the position, company, job number and date as your first line.

Example:

YOUR LETTERHEAD HERE
(same as your résumé)

Date

Company and Address

Attention: Rod Adams, Human Resources

Dear Rod,

RE: Senior Marketing Specialist Application, Reference No. 2007-221

I am writing in response to the posting on your website for a Senior Marketing Specialist (Reference No. 2007-221). As a highly motivated individual, the challenges and rewards of this position appeal greatly to me, and I look forward to bringing my proven marketing, community relations and leadership success to ABC Oil & Gas Company Limited.

Highlights of my accomplishments developed during my tenure as Director and Manager at SAS Media include:

- Proven history of successfully managing multiple projects simultaneously resulting in financial expectations and event goals met or exceeded
- Successfully implemented market development strategies resulting in 10% year-on-year growth in a developing market
- Successfully fostering community relations by initiating and developing relationships with strategic non-profit and charitable organizations resulting in higher profiles and increased sales for their projects as well as increased visibility and good will for SAS Media
- Strong team building, coaching and leadership skills resulting in all direct reports winning company awards and recognition

My résumé and references are attached. I look forward to meeting with you at your convenience to discuss my qualifications.

Best regards,

Sue Li

Enc. Résumé and references

When Sue gleaned tremendous in-depth information about the energy company's IT department from reading and talking to people, she summarized the highlights in her cover letter. After reading Sue's letter, the CEO called her in for an interview the next day. Sue is now the Manager of Information Technology Solutions at one of the top five energy companies. She had no prior energy experience before she secured this position.

REQUEST FOR INFORMATIONAL MEETING LETTER

This introduction letter is merely an expanded form of your pitch and includes the essential elements to get you a meeting or an interview.

Start by writing out your pitch, adding a few paragraphs as follows:

1. State your purpose for writing

The first paragraph tells them why you are writing. This paragraph should be focused on the receiver and will include two parts.

2. Supply your reference first

If you have a reference, start off the letter with something like: "Joe Smith, Manager of Operations at Telus Mobility, suggested I write to you because of your knowledge of project management in the oil and gas industry."

3. Then add gems from your research

Next, provide information about the individual and/or their company. This will show you have done your research. Has their company won an award for their annual report? Did they develop a state-of-the-art tracking system for project management? Are they building or currently researching upgraders? Do they sit on the Board of Directors for an energy trust and a production company and therefore have great insight into the industry?

4. State the information you are seeking

In the second paragraph, state the information that you understand to be true about their organization. Give a brief example(s) of a solution(s) to a problem they may be facing. (ie: "With careful review of your latest annual report, I have noted that your main objective for the next year is to expand into the Middle East. My extensive network in that region would support your organization's goals.")

5. Add credibility and sparkle

Now give them motivation to want to meet you. You have already impressed them by the in-depth information you have about their company. Start off with a summary statement. (ie: "Over the last two years, I have been successful at introducing an environmental firm to key contacts in the Middle East, resulting in 120% per year growth for my client.")

6. Call to action

Your next step is to request a meeting. Honour how busy they are and suggest a meeting at their convenience, some time in the next few weeks. Offer to bring a coffee to their office or ask if they'd prefer to meet outside their office.

Then take responsibility for the next action step. Say you will follow-up with them within one week unless you hear from them first.

If you have a strong reference and have presented compelling research about the company, there is a good chance the person will either respond with a meeting time, or refer you to an appropriate person within the company.

PROPOSAL LETTERS

A proposal letter can be written after you have had your "informational" meeting and have a clear understanding of the employer's situation and needs. In other words, when you know exactly what is keeping him up at night.

Start off by referencing your past meeting(s). Then move on to **define the company's business problem or challenge that you discussed** when you met and studied further through additional research on the topic. To write this type of letter effectively, you must step into the decision maker's shoes. If you get this "problem definition" part right, the decision maker will be convinced you understand his situation and will want to read further.

In the next paragraphs, describe yourself as the solution to the problem, showing how your skills and expertise can help address the company's needs. Go into as much detail as you need to illustrate you are well matched to meet this challenge and you're confident the solution you propose cannot fail. **Describe the specific actions you will take, showing you have a definite plan and a firm foundation of knowledge and expertise, backed up with past successes with similar challenges.**

A recommended approach is to propose your services with a specific and definable project. This will give you an opportunity to demonstrate your high-quality work, with minimal risk to the company.

Be sure your letter clearly states the benefit to the decision maker in considering your offer. When he or she asks, "so what's in it for me or for my company," the answer should jump off the page.

Don't forget to **end your letter with a call to action.** Offer to give a presentation to key stakeholders and take responsibility for follow-up.

FOLLOW-UP LETTERS

When following-up with a new contact in writing, be sure to review your connection and briefly summarize your communication thus far. Express appreciation, highlighting anything you want to expand upon based on your last communication. Then outline how you will follow through on the contact's suggestions and advice. Try to think of ways to give back to this person. If you run across an interesting article, for example, enclose it alongside your letter.

Example:

Date

Company and Address

Attention: Name and Title

Dear Robert,

RE: Follow-up to our meeting (date)

Thank you for meeting with me last Friday and for providing such an interesting perspective regarding your booming industry. I'm attaching a recent Harvard Business Review article that echoes your views.

As we discussed, I am interested in securing a middle management costing or accounting position. With my depth of experience, I believe I can make a positive contribution to a company in need of a professional with my skills.

Following your suggestion, I plan to contact Walter White and Tanya Hicks this week, and I will advise you of the outcome of my discussions with both. I would appreciate your keeping me apprised of other contacts that may come to mind, and I will keep you updated on my progress.

Again, thank you for sharing your valuable time and expertise.

Best wishes,

Rodney Brown

Attachment: article

THANK YOU LETTERS

Expressing appreciation is important during all phases of your job search. Thank you letters or cards can be sent after meetings, interviews or even useful phone conversations.

Your thank you will be remembered and will help you to stand out and be noticed. **It's very important to be specific in your thanks and express what it was the person said or did that has been of particular benefit.**

General rules on letter writing

- Keep the letter brief, using small easy-to-read paragraphs
- Stick to one page for cover letters and up to three pages maximum for proposal letters
- Use bullets whenever possible to capture accomplishments
- Have a few people read your letter to ensure perfect grammar and spelling
- Read the letter out loud to make sure it makes sense
- Use an easily readable font and font size
- Use the same letterhead on all your documentation
- If the letter is being mailed, use good quality paper

LAST WORD:
STAY ON TOP OF CHANGE AND KEEP YOUR FACTS STRAIGHT

The world is in a constant state of flux. Never assume that yesterday's news is still applicable today. Departments, divisions, players and titles – everything can change in an instant.

Cat's Tale

I learned this truth the hard way when I attended a function at my landlord's old-time saloon in the mountains. I was innocently chatting with a woman about the beautiful scenery surrounding us and about the woman's passion for social work. When the conversation turned to my business, the woman mentioned that her husband also worked in the energy industry. I introduced myself to the woman's husband, who told me the name of the company he worked for. When I asked what his role was, he said he was the president. Disbelievingly, I practically shouted, "No, you're not!" (I had met the president a few weeks earlier, and this was definitely not that man!) "Well yes, actually, I am," he replied. It turned out, he had accepted the president's position just days earlier.

The new president graciously overlooked my blunder, and they shared a good laugh. But I have never made that mistake again. Nor should you.

Before sending out correspondence or meeting with new contacts, be sure you have your facts straight.

NOTES

Cat's Tips to Get the Job of Your Dreams

CHAPTER FOUR

NETWORKING IS
THE NEW BLACK

"Striving for success without hard work is like trying to harvest where you have not planted."
David Bly, Desert News, Salt Lake City

THE ART OF NETWORKING

You never know who you are going to meet at a networking event. In fact, we believe that each and every person you meet is equally important.

First impressions. Everybody knows how important first impressions are. But not everybody knows that the "first impression" is actually only a **seven- second** window. (www.businessinsider.com)

Dress to impress. This does not mean you must break the bank on the latest fashion trends. You must, however, coordinate your outfit with precision and thought.

Dress for the position you desire, not the one you already have. All great fashion consultants will advise on investing in at least one key piece of clothing per season, and mixing this piece with your existing wardrobe.

Consignment and thrift stores vary in quality; every major centre has them. If you know where the high-income earners live in a metropolitan area, chances are excellent that consignment stores in those areas will carry some of this season's and last season's most popular pieces for a fraction of the retail (or original) cost.

Stay healthy in every way. Times of transition can be the most stressful time of your life. Try to carve out at least 10 minutes every day to nurture your health and well-being: go for a walk, play with your kids or your pets, work out, enjoy your sport, practice yoga, meditate or ponder over a cup of tea in the sunshine, run a hot bath, weed your garden … you get the idea. Whatever this activity is, it should bring you a sense of calm and self-reward. Without planning, these are the first activities to fall away and the most challenging ones to re-establish. **Make this a commitment and part of your daily routine.** Look at this time as an investment in resisting negative energy. We spoke about this in our "Prepping for Breakthrough" chapter; the energy we emit resonates with those around us.

Nutrition is another very important element of staying healthy. Make careful choices in how you nourish your body. The quality of food you ingest will affect your level of energy.

Stay positive by resisting the tendency to be negative when stress is high.

When in the company of all others, maintain a positive vibe. The more positive communications you have with those around you, the more your body's positive energy permeates your surroundings and mirrors back on you. It's true! This really works!

Pick two people in your life you can vent and flare with and whom you trust. Establish an agreement to ignite your cause to offload and release the burning matter. The promise is that the rant will last no more than three minutes maximum. Once you've vented, together reframe the situation:

What did you just learn from this situation?

How do you move forward with this matter?

What steps can you establish to remain positive?

Mentors. Identify mentors in all aspects of your life. These are people you may already receive guidance from. Nurture these valuable ties. In addition to these, source new ones! They do not need to be people you know personally. Aside from hands-on learning, guidance and growing your network, one of the largest benefits to mentoring is the development of new peers. Peer sharing creates reciprocity, stronger bonds, builds trust and future business successes.

Look around you – that means outside your industry too – for people of varying cultures and backgrounds, different belief systems and expansive age groups. These are places for you to ask a lot of questions and learn. **Always ask how you can offer support either in their community or on their road to success.**

One of Catherine's colleagues, Stan Peake, of InSite Performance Coaching, believes that your visible work ethic and attitude will prove your own worth as a potential mentee. He claims mentorship does not come with assumed entitlement, rather it is up to you to show that your commitment to lifelong learning is a priority. While some professionals will formally ask those they aspire to for mentorship, he believes that at least as often are the cases in which a mentor sees the potential in a hard-working mentee and the process begins organically.

If you read CBI's newsletters, you already know that one of Catherine's favourite mentors is Marie Forleo, who has her own online TV channel. (www.marieforleo.com/marietv)

Below are six points Forleo attests to excellence in mentorship:

1. **You don't necessarily need to meet your mentor.** With access to infinite online podcasts, media and learning sources, you can establish mentors that influence you in virtually every corner of the world!

2. **Be a *polymentorist*:** Seek not one mentor, but many. Source mentors in all aspects of your life and interests to help grow your skills, knowledge bases, confidence and network.

3. **Don't always look up for a mentor,** look sideways, too. The power in having a colleague as a mentor establishes your mutual values, shared skills and opportunity to learn from their mistakes (and save you time and frustration).

4. **Be specific, not vague.** Ask your mentor specific questions, rather than generalized ones.

5. **Earn respect and trust through actions.** Show genuine support to your mentor by endorsing the matters that are important to her (ie: attend a function, buy her book, offer to assist) and do so without an agenda.

6. **Do great work in the world.** Focus on always achieving quality, results, care and consistency ... in everything you do!

Be well versed on global trends. With technology at your fingertips, you have every reason to be informed about what is happening in the world. Remember you are not required to have an opinion, but to share a tidbit of knowledge that may spark interest in others. This is the best place to ask questions, and perhaps learn more about a new topic. **You will know when your opinion is of any interest when you are asked.**

Learning as a lifelong event. The world is changing exponentially each and every moment of the day. University degrees become outdated very quickly. Being the best at your craft means being on the crest of the learning wave. This does not necessarily require going back to school, but many professionals prioritize attaining more credentials as a desired (and often required) method of career advancement. Some organizations will even fund your educational efforts. There are also creative ways to fit learning into your busy schedule, such as listening to an audiobook or a podcast instead of music during your commute.

PROFESSIONAL AFFILIATIONS

Many professionals choose other ways to keep their edges sharply honed:

- Join the affiliation that aligns with your specific industry or profession
- Buy memberships (or affiliate memberships) that support these organizations or their causes
- By mentoring less-experienced colleagues in your line of work, you will be aware of how learning has changed and how these factors influence your current and future successes
- Become an expert in your field by reading new and novel angles of old technologies or processes
- Volunteering with the association where you will meet future colleagues will be beneficial to building your network

SERVE AND SUPPORT

In some parts of the world, there is a large percentage of community-minded leaders who volunteer their time to support those around them. Find something you are passionate about. Offer your greatest skill set and connect with like-minded individuals, who, over time, you can add to your "Love Army™." More on what a "Love Army™" is and how to make it work for you in the chapters that follow.

Cat's Tip

When you are in network mode, you are not looking for a job. You are there to build relationships and find a place to serve others.

You will know it is your time to talk when you are asked to.

NETWORKING EVENTS

Set an Intention. Before a networking event, give yourself a goal or set an intention. Prior to attending, ascertain if the purpose of the event is to initiate or grow your network. This will remind you that the time invested is valuable. You are less likely to hang around chatting with those you already know, if you keep this notion present.

For those who are more introverted, try reframing networking events from a 'necessary evil' to an opportunity. How much would you pay to skip the résumé pile and get face time with the president of the company? That may be exactly what you are doing for free at your next networking event!

"Change your thoughts and you change your world."
Reverend Norman Vincent Peale

Some goals may include the following:

- Connect with **three new contacts** at a deep enough level that you feel confident that you have new friends
- Find **one thing about each person** that makes them unique and memorable
- Find one thing you can do **to serve and support**
- Make every **conversation all about the person** you are meeting

Business cards: Never leave home without them!

When Catherine meets someone for the first time and they share their business card with her, she has already learned something about the person she is meeting, before any words have been exchanged.

This is your calling card and must show well each and every time.

Distributing quality business cards is as important as how you dress – first impressions are lasting!

Cat's Tip

Your business card should include:

- A description of your discipline or specialty – in three words or less
- Crisp, quality card stock – applying colours and designs that are appropriate for your profession
- Use legible font and remember to leave white space
- Carry your cards in a holder to ensure they are not bent, discoloured or marred in any way
- If someone you meet does not have a card, write their coordinates on the back of one of yours so you can follow-up later
- Order a small batch at first and trial them before committing to a more affordable, larger volume (many local printers and online services offer discounts for large orders)
- Never use cards with perforated edges

Develop a system when handing out your cards at events. Perhaps wear an outfit with pockets with cards you dispense in the right pocket, those you receive in the left. For women, you may assign a similar system using your handbag, or carry a palm-size card folder or wallet. Handing out someone else's card in error, or having to cross the room to retrieve your card wastes time and looks less than organized.

Name tags. If a function supplies nametags, make sure you wear one. We recommend placing it below your right shoulder so, when you meet a new face and shake hands, your tag is easy to read.

Bring a pen. Sometimes there may be key information for you to recall following (or during) a conversation. Using your electronic device to make notes can be perceived as distracted and insincere, and also requires you to lose eye contact.

Alcohol consumption and **smoking** are worth mentioning too. Consider your ability to maintain a level of professional disposition, regardless of culture or protocols.

Food is often served at network events, but can also be a detriment. We recommend eating something before you go so that you can focus on the event, rather than the edibles. Remember, if you cannot shake hands, or your mouth is too full to have a conversation, your first impression may be less than impressive.

Buddy up. Not everyone is comfortable carving out fresh new conversations with strangers. If this describes you, then invite an extroverted friend to come along to a networking event. You can join conversations that you're comfortable with and grow your confidence at your own pace.

Positive attitudes rule! Regardless of your personal views on a topic, the best policy to impart a good impression is to reserve negativity for another time. (Refer to the **Cat's Tool** earlier in this chapter about venting and flaring.)

Mirroring. This is the behaviour by which one person consciously imitates the gesture, speech pattern or attitude of another. This often occurs in social situations and builds rapport. At the subconscious level, people feel less intimidated, more at ease and equal when conversing with someone who is 'similar' to them. Successful mirroring starts from the very first moment we meet someone and shake their hand: where possible, a web-to-web handshake is highly recommended. However, there will be situations that require a different approach, depending on culture or the possibility of meeting someone with a hand injury.

The pitch. Your pitch is a quick summarization of who you are and what you've accomplished in your career, including your objectives. It is a crucial and effective tool to your networking success. You will know your own pitch very well because you will have practiced it many times and you will be prepared to present it when you are asked about what you do. We will expand on the key elements of your pitch in the next chapter.

Reciprocity. A successful networker knows the value of asking questions. Your ability to focus on those you meet will become integral to your success in building a new relationship. Learn how you can assist the person in some way or benefit them.

Cat's Tip

> Following the event, take some time to jot a note on each business card that you collected:
> - Date
> - Interesting fact or what is unique about them
> - Code the card according to your needs (ie: request a meeting, refer to another person, etc.)
> - Then follow-up within 48 hours of the event by connecting through social media and sending a note to them directly
> - Or take a photo of the business card and email it to yourself with highlights of your conversation

One-liners. They do hold value. People attend networking events to meet others and grow their networks too. In these situations, one-liners are a means to start conversations and learn more about those you are meeting.

Here are a few good examples:
- How do you know the host/hostess?
- What motivated you to attend this event?
- Do you belong to a volunteer organization?
- Do you have a career you enjoy?
- Is there anything I can do to support you?
- May I give you my business card?

Here are some to avoid:
- Do you have a job for me?

- Can I send you my résumé?

After the intro. Once you've established a rapport, we recommend asking questions that allow you to go deeper. Here are some recommendations:

- What do you do for fun?
- What are you currently doing in the world of work?
- What's the best part about your role?
- What's been your greatest accomplishment?
- What sort of challenges do you face?
- What organizations outside of work do you belong to?
- What are your objectives for attending this event?
- Do you participate in any leisure activities?
- Does the organization where you volunteer need new members?

Each one of these questions is a threshold for expansion. Remember, the focus of the conversation should be on the person you are meeting and not on you.

Cat's Tip

> Catherine recommends Jim Collins' book, *Good to Great*, where he explains the "5 Whys" that will build solid and positive relationships. In short, asking 'why' up to five times, five different ways helps to go from a more 'surface' response to a deeper understanding of what motivates the person you are talking to.

Keep fluid. Allow yourself enough time to make a meaningful connection. Before leaving the conversation, thank your new friend for his time and let him know that you will send a social media invitation and invite him for coffee in the next few weeks.

Relax and be yourself. Some events can be stressful. Learning how to approach these events feeling open and relaxed make them enjoyable.

"If you focus on your curiosity and genuine interest in the other person, you won't have time to be nervous, self-conscious, awkward, self-critical, or anything else. You will be too busy being interested in them."

www.TheGoGiver.com

Cat's Tip

DO: Use your breath to carry you through the space from one thought to the other.

DO: avoid unconfident words when filling space; "Uhm" "Ah" "So" "As well as ..."

DO: Minimize the use of the word "but" so as not to detract from the value of what you just stated. "But" has the tendency to override everything that just preceded it.

DO: Tell the truth, but avoid saying "To tell you the truth ..." Similar to "but," this phrase has a tendency to suggest dishonesty.

Eye contact: Give it freely and directly. However, keep in mind that where we are in the world matters when it comes to eye contact. Different cultures may view eye contact as a form of aggression.

Listen up: This empowering skill will provide you with a distinctive advantage in so many professional situations. Good listeners have the ability to reiterate and mirror what is important to others. Hearing what others say makes the speaker feel important, validated and acknowledged.

Follow-up within 48 hours. These steps are critical to your success:

• Send an invitation through social media to connect

- Send a personal note that reminds your new friend of the conversation you had and invite them to meet in the next several weeks
- Send them relevant information when you come across something you think they might be interested in
- If you made any promises at the event, ensure you follow through with them
- Building rapport provides the opportunity to stay in touch **6 times, 6 different ways, over 6 months** ("**6x6x6**"™)

"All the time and effort put into networking can be all for naught if there is no follow-through. The same goes for sales. And leadership. And well, everything."

Beth Ramsay

NOTES

CHAPTER FIVE

PERFECTING THE PITCH

"First impressions matter. Experts say we size up new people in somewhere between 30 seconds and two minutes."

Elliott Abrams,
American Diplomat, Lawyer and Politcal Scientist

One of the most powerful tools you will develop as you transition your career is what we call your "pitch." This super-brief summary about you must be developed and applied in every setting to introduce yourself to individuals and groups, as well as to prospective employers, clients and future friends.

THE PITCH

Purpose: Your personal pitch is an impromptu opportunity for you to express a quick summary of who you are, what sets you apart from your competition, and to entice your listener to ask questions and learn more about you.

Three main components:

1. **Who you are:**   Why should they listen to you?

2. **What you do:**   What are you an expert at, or passionate about?

3. **Who you serve:**   How do you apply your unique skill set?

Here are some examples of **pitch foundations** developed by some of our friends:

> Catherine: "I am a 30-year entrepreneur, passionate about connecting people and organizations across the globe who I believe in. I look forward to applying my expertise and experience to international community development."

> Stan: "I am a business and performance coach driven to help triple bottom line focused leaders maximize their potential and their returns."

> Karen: "I am an entrepreneur with over 40 years business experience, specializing in customer service, administration and bookkeeping. I'm passionate about helping my clients' businesses be efficient and cost-effective. I'm seeking clients who are fun to work with and who will challenge me to learn new skills."

> Liane: "Over the past decade I've developed my skills in the areas of writing, editing, publishing and language. I empower others to maximize their messages with minimal words, the results of which bring clarity and advancement."

Here are even tighter versions (**perfected pitches**) that will leave the listener wanting more:

Catherine: "I connect people across the globe that I believe in – and sometimes I make money at it. I look forward to serving and supporting."

Stan: "I help values-based leaders gain the peace of mind to sleep better at night and the inspiration to wake up the next day ready to make their dreams a reality."

Karen: "With my extensive background in customer service, administration and bookkeeping, I am the Miss Moneypenny, working behind the scenes to help my clients achieve their missions."

Liane: "My passion for perfecting the spoken and written message has helped both me and those with whom I collaborate to achieve clarity and voice."

MAKE IT YOURS

In our networking events we routinely help professionals craft and hone their pitches. Sometimes it's a tweak here, an edit there, or a few word suggestions. Other times, it's a complete overhaul or cutting 90% of "the fluff" to focus on "the meat." In any case, however polished, professional, or intriguing a pitch may sound, it has to be something you can make authentically yours.

One of our attendee's first attempts at her pitch was something like the following;

"My name is Beth (not her real name) and I have a 15-year history in engineering. I have received a lot of recognition for my ability to improve processes and systems, and I have a very analytical approach to project management and implementation. My superiors are always fond of my work and they have mentioned that I help make their jobs easier. I am also very attentive to budgets, timelines, and resources as I implement better systems and processes."

It was actually a lot longer than that, but you get the point. One suggestion to simplify her pitch was, "CEO's love me because I think processes are sexy." The whole room cheered and thought our suggestion "nailed it" – except for Beth! Extremely introverted, proper, and professional – this was something she could never own with confidence. Once we knew this about Beth, the pitch was refined and became "I help make executives' lives easier by supporting them with seamless processes."

In summary, no matter how good your pitch looks on paper, it has to be YOUR pitch – you have to be able to say it confidently, authentically and with authority.

PRACTICE, PRACTICE, PRACTICE!

Once you have secured the three components, you will become adept at altering your content as required. Your pitch will become more comfortable the more you practice it. It will be important to create several different pitches, depending on where you are and with whom you are connecting. Be ready to change it on the fly.

Your pitch should be practiced enough to be top of mind and conversationally roll off your tongue, but not so rehearsed that you come across robotic or "salesy" (even if you are selling).

NO HISTORY PLEASE

When people are asked what they do, they typically tell the history of how they arrived where they are today. Do not do this! Keep your conversation forward moving and positive.

Imagine you ask someone why he's at the biker club gathering and he rambles on about how he used to ride a Honda, but it got boring and now he'd really like to find a Harley. No!

It is better to start with the future in a specific way ... "I'm looking for a 1961 Harley-Davidson," or "I'm looking for a job in human resources in energy," or "I'm looking for information about sales and marketing in energy supply companies."

STAY POSITIVE

We encourage you to keep your entire conversation with contacts and future employers positive – especially when you talk about your previous employment. Otherwise, you will represent yourself as a negative person.

Choosing the right tone:

- "I work in the post office. If I stay there any longer I think I'll go postal."

    - This could be transformed to, "I have loved working with the post office. I have honed my interpersonal skills and work ethic and am excited about getting into oil and gas because..."

- "I'm a chiropractor. If I crack another bone I'm going to scream."

    - This could be transformed to, "I have dedicated myself to training and wellness for 15 years in my profession as a chiropractor. Now I am excited about bringing my training abilities into energy."

- "I own my own business and spend too much time alone."

    - This could be transformed to, "I have honed my business skills and grown my bottom line by 20% each year for the past 10 years. I would like to bring my sales savvy to an oil and gas service company."

BE CREATIVE

Most people we encounter entirely miss the opportunity to open new conversations by bypassing their pitch altogether. Instead of "I help values-based leaders gain the peace of mind to sleep better at night and the inspiration to wake up the next day ready to make their dreams a reality," they simply open with "my name is Stan and I am a business coach." To help you move away from 'name and position' introductions, here are a few more clever pitches to consider.

Title	Creative Pitch
• Carpenter	"I build dream homes"
• Dentist	"I'm in the smile business"
• Jeweller	"I've been getting the girls next door gala-ready since 1997"
• Accountant	"I teach people to save $5000 in taxes in 45 minutes"
• Server	"I'm a professional conversationalist who sometimes goes over the dinner special"

ALL ABOUT YOUR AUDIENCE

Your pitch is very brief for a good reason: the rest of the conversation should be focused on finding out about the other person:

- Where does he work?
- What does she like about her role?
- What are the challenges?
- What is he proud of?
- How did she get her first job in the energy sector?

Most people naturally love to talk about themselves. While asking them questions and listening carefully to their answers, you are gathering important information you can apply in creating your own future. Be genuine and view each person you meet as a fascinating resource for your growth.

Tip: Try to engage whoever you are talking to through questions first. Most people are more willing to listen to you after you have listened to them. By showing genuine interest in who they are, they will become more interested to learn more about you.

THE GOAL

Even if you are looking for a job, or trying to land a new client, your pitch is not a sales proposition or call to action to hire you. **The goal of your pitch is to ignite a conversation.** The likelihood of being hired or contracted based on your opening statement is virtually zero. A clever, well-crafted pitch however, can open a conversation by grabbing the client or hiring manager's genuine interest. If they are genuinely interested in you at the onset of a conversation, you have the opportunity to tell your story and they will see you for the worthy candidate you are.

The more interested they are on the way into a conversation, the more likely they will remember you afterwards, which multiples your chances of moving through the candidacy process towards hiring (or sales channel through landing the client)!

DID YOU NAIL IT?

As mentioned, the goal of your pitch is to ignite a conversation. We use the word "ignite" deliberately to convey emotion and enthusiasm, in the same way we say to someone who is on a roll, "you're on fire!"

This means there is some excitement to the conversation! One way you can tell whether or not your pitch worked is by the type of questions you get in response. No questions often means no interest. "I'm sorry, what do you do again?" Means that your pitch wasn't clear.

Questions like "how do you do that?" or "how long have you done that?" or "where did you learn to do that?" indicate interest, even enthusiasm.

Occasionally, you'll even hit a home run and hear someone respond, "Oh, you need to meet my friend John. He needs someone just like you to help him with (insert your clever pitch here!)."

NOTES

CHAPTER SIX

SOCIAL MEDIA

"If you're not on Social Media, how can we find you?"

Catherine Brownlee, Global Headhunter

Social media is one of the most effective means to conduct business and reach your network. Some platforms offer more benefits than others in growing your contacts and making you accessible worldwide. Regardless of which platform you feel is most effective, online is where you will be researched prior to anyone reaching out to or connecting with you.

> Use discernment with what you say, post, like and dislike, and be cautious with whom you align your profile. Always remember that your background, views and values (and those you are associated with) are being researched and evaluated in advance of you being contacted.

LINKEDIN

LinkedIn is the most powerful online business tools and is used by recruiters around the world. Typically, it is the first database recruiters go to when searching for any type of candidate. It is a valuable platform for you to make a positive first impression to recruiters, clients and colleagues. Therefore, it is extremely important that your profile is at "all star" level, with the following included:

- Photo: include a professional headshot showing you dressed for success. Smile! You're being watched. The visual detection market is expanding tremendously. Emotion recognition takes mere facial detection/recognition a step further and it will be important to ensure your photo reflects you in a positive light.

- Be sure to include all content from your résumé.

- Summary: Your name, email address, phone number, website (if applicable), needs to be on the first line of the summary in your profile. If you have developed a great "pitch" or tag line, you may want to consider including it in this section.

- Ensure that all of your skills are checked off in the skills area. Ask your friends and colleagues to endorse the skills they have witnessed.

- When seeking recommendations from your contacts, it will be valuable for you to request them through LinkedIn. This will make it easy for your contact to 'Write Recommendation' and it gives you the opportunity to review their recommendation prior to posting on your profile. Recruiters and Hiring Managers always review your full LinkedIn profile, and especially the recommendations from your contacts. It will serve you well to have as many as possible for public review.

- Connect with contacts and send them a personal note saying that you look forward to staying in touch. If there is a call to action to meet or to be introduced to someone in their network, this is the perfect time.

- A very effective way to request an introduction is through your first-person connections to theirs. Both full LinkedIn profiles are revealed to one another and you have made it easy for your first connection to write the introduction and recommend an informational meeting.

There are tools you can use to scrape your LinkedIn profile to build a résumé or profile. However, this should not replace a professionally constructed résumé, but rather be used more as a great calling card.

Cat's Tool

Spend the time required to ensure your profile is at 100% or "All Star." All of the details in your résumé should be transferred to your profile page, including all paid and volunteer roles, education and professional development and affiliations.

Make sure that people can contact you, either via LinkedIn or your personal email.

Have a professional headshot done. Never post a photo on LinkedIn that was taken while performing a leisure activity. Keep it professional.

Take the time and invest in LinkedIn training (in person or online) to maximize this powerful tool.

FACEBOOK

As with all other social media platforms, opinions will be formed by readers of your online Facebook profile. We recommend adding a privacy filter that will allow only those you select to view your wall. Always use discernment with your posts, especially where delicate topics are showcased (ie: politics, religion, racial and gender topics). We know of cases where recruiters decided not to interview a qualified candidate for a position after having toured their social media venues.

If you decide that you wish to be completely unfiltered on Facebook, you would be wise to check and sensor your account daily while you are in the career search mode. We urge you not to post photos where you are holding or consuming an adult beverage or smoking.

YOUTUBE

YouTube is another fine example of a successful social media platform. Anyone can create a YouTube account and, provided the content meets an agreeable level of censorship, can be broadcast on your station throughout the world. Again, use discernment.

TWITTER

Twitter is an excellent way to endorse people and organizations with whom you share similarities, or whose mandates you find valuable and meaningful. It is also a great way to keep up on current topics, receive up-to-the-minute releases and effortlessly share your findings with your own network.

Unlike Facebook, where you must approve a new friend, Twitter simply informs you of a new follower. You can block those you feel are not suitable, and you should if you are concerned that having an inappropriate follower could jeopardize your reputation.

INSTAGRAM

Instagram is not just for selfies or pictures of your lunch!

Depending on the type of work you are looking for, your Instagram account may act as a sort of online portfolio. This would be an obvious platform to maximize for an aspiring photographer, but what about an aspiring adventure guide? Posting pictures of your coolest hikes, kayaking adventures, or other treks would be a great way to show a potential employer that this is your lifestyle and that you know your stuff!

Other professionals who may be able to leverage Instagram to build their careers include chefs (if your finished product is drool-inducing, you are well on your way!), carpenters (even your recreational projects may catch the eye of a contractor or employer), and public speakers or comedians (you on stage in front of an audience is an instant credibility builder).

NOTES

CHAPTER SEVEN

GROW WHO YOU KNOW

"There are no strangers here;
only friends you haven't yet met."

William Butler Yeats

This chapter talks about the importance of expanding your network. Positive results will come with commitment and practice.

BUILDING YOUR LOVE ARMY™

Catherine began using this technique when she worked at McGavin Foods early in her sales career. Her boss and mentor, Tim Fesik, taught her everything she needed to know about sales and high-touch client service. This method worked to grow her sales results and build her businesses over the years that followed.

Reaching your target involves a simple formula. Start with the people who know and love you (we call them your "Love Army™"). Ask them for information, referrals and advice in the area or industry you are interested in pursuing. It is important to realize that every person you meet along this route will be critical to your journey.

STEP ONE:

Start with the list of people who love you (your **Love Army™**). List them all – the people you can contact and ask for a one-hour meeting that will be all about you: Mom, uncle, sister, next door neighbour, yoga instructor ... all of them. Let your Love Army™ know what you are trying to attract for yourself. You are seeking their information, referrals and advice. Say "Yes" to all referrals that are given to you as opportunities to grow your network. Over time, expect up to five referrals from everyone in your Love Army™.

You control the process! In most cases, your Love Army™ will want to make the introduction. Thank them for the referral and tell them you will make the initial contact and mention their name. By taking this step out of their hands, you show initiative and avoid the possibility that they might get busy with their week and forget.

Use an Excel spreadsheet or CRM for a visual tracking system of your "**Grow Who You Know™**" process, procedure and success (see sample on next page).

GROW WHO YOU KNOW™

Your Love Army™	Referral	Receptionist	Date of Contact	Method of Contact	Follow-up Date #1	Follow-up Date #2	Follow-up Date #3	Introductory Meeting Date	Referral, etc.	6 Times, 6 Different Ways, Over 6 Months

Cat's Tale

When I was Marketing Administrator for a mall in Calgary, I was responsible for planning a Stampede BBQ. We wanted all proceeds to go to a children's charity and, with that in mind, I started approaching suppliers to obtain the BBQ products for free.

The general manager at the bread company I approached was next to impossible to reach. I left several messages before actually connecting with him one day by phone.

He insisted I be brief. Fortunately, I had practiced the spiel so many times that I could summarize what I needed inside of two minutes. He said he could sell us product at cost but that he was unable to give it away for free. I told him that it was for a charity and his company could benefit with signage and a charity tax receipt. He told me he would think about it and discuss the idea with his vice president, but this kind of thing was typically not done at his company. He asked that I call him again in two days.

I phoned back in two days and left a message. In fact, I left messages every two days for the next two weeks. When he finally took my call, he said he had an update for me but was in the middle of something. Would I mind holding? I held. For 45 minutes in fact.

When he came back on the line; he said, "Hello; who is this? Oh ... are you still there?" He said very well then, I could pick up the free product that afternoon at 5:00 p.m. Fabulous. I would send a maintenance man with our company truck. "No," he said. "If you want the product, you will have to come pick it up yourself."

Big issue for me! I still had so much to finish before the upcoming function. Of course I agreed and arrived at his office with our truck at 4:45 p.m. I waited in his reception area while all of his staff left the building for the day – it turned out to be another 45 minutes.

When he finally stepped out of his office to greet me, he said, "You're still here? Let's talk." He wanted to know if I'd ever considered sales? Coming from the marketing side of the business, sales seemed to me to be too much like "Herb Tarlek" from WKRP. I told him that marketing was more of a love for me and off I went, product in hand, to frantically get ready for the BBQ.

Somewhere throughout this experience, the tables had definitely turned. The general manager wooed me for the next two months, and we negotiated our way to my future career in sales at McGavins. I stayed with his company for over two years. The manager turned out to be an excellent mentor for me and I am forever grateful. It was a great training ground for everything to follow in my life.

STEP TWO:

Do your research on the individual and their organization prior to contacting them. Check them out on the Internet, LinkedIn, company web page, annual report and press releases.

Place the collected data in a file folder with the name of the person you are hoping to meet. When you do get that appointment, they will be impressed to see that file in your hands.

STEP THREE:

Plan your telephone communication for a time that will most likely be received positively:

- Avoid their first day of work after the weekend or holiday. They will be catching up from being away and may not want to be distracted.

- The best day is their second workday in the afternoon.

- Mornings between 7:30 a.m. and 8:30 a.m. before they get their day started is also good.

- The last day of their workweek between 1:30 p.m. and the end of that day is also a good time for many. When we are attempting to connect with decision makers, they typically remain in their office to continue motivating their team. They, too, are thinking about the weekend and are more open to having an initial, non-pressured conversation.

Leaving a telephone message
- Strive for a friendly, positive tone
- Pronounce your name clearly, both at the beginning and end of your message
- Slow down when giving your telephone number and repeat it twice
- Stand while talking (this helps you to project your voice and exude confidence)
- Smile when speaking (this helps to keep your tone light and positive)

Email and LinkedIn messaging are suitable at any time and allow the recipient to respond on their own time.

First Call

Catherine prefers to use the 'old school method' of phoning. In her seminars, she shares these tips as follows:

(Calling the main reception line on Tuesday afternoon at about 1:30 p.m.)

Ring, ring ...

"Hello, my name is Catherine Brownlee and I am interested in connecting with Sarah Smith; would she be in her office? ... Oh, thank you ... and sorry, I did not catch your name?.....

James, thank you James. Voicemail will be fine."

"Hi Sarah, my name is Catherine Brownlee and my mom, Clare Brownlee, referred your name to me and spoke so highly of you. Sarah, I have reviewed your successful career and philanthropic efforts online and I am very interested to learn more about you and your accomplishments. I would be happy to bring your favourite beverage to your office in the next several weeks, at your convenience. If we can connect over a short meeting, I would be extremely grateful to learn more. My phone number is 403-861-2001 and I will send you a note through LinkedIn in the event it may be easier to respond at your convenience. Thank you Sarah, I will follow-up within one week to ensure receipt of my voicemail."

STEP FOUR:

Record your call on your Grow Who You Know™ tool (Excel spreadsheet, CRM database, etc.).

Keep a running check of your promises to return calls, attend invitations to meet, coffee dates, etc. Be precise, attentive and diligent with your commitments.

Cat's Tip

Second Call

On the date promised in the initial communication, make your second call:

"Good morning. Oh, is this James? It's Catherine Brownlee calling. How is your day so far? Yes, that's correct, I'm trying to connect with Sarah. No, I do not mind being put on hold."

"Oh, I understand she is busy. That's not a problem. I'm impressed at your professionalism, James. I used to be a receptionist early in my career and I failed miserably. Your skills are exceptional!"

"I would be happy to leave another voicemail, if you don't mind patching me through. But before you do, I plan to be in your area next week and would love to stop by and introduce myself. Oh, great! See you next week." (Be sure to record the date promised.)

Leave Sarah a voicemail:

"Hi Sarah, it's Catherine Brownlee again. I left a voicemail a week ago. I know you are extremely busy. I'm not sure you received it. After researching your career and philanthropic efforts, I am extremely impressed and would like the opportunity to learn more. I have sent you a note through LinkedIn and you will be able to see my profile online."

"My phone number is 403-861-2001 if there is an opportunity to connect on the phone. I will follow-up in another week and see if I can reach you then. Have a wonderful day!"

Back to the Grow Who You Know™ tool:

Mark down this day's mode of communication with Sarah, and that you connected with James again.

The next step is extremely important!

Again, follow through with your promises. Do whatever you stated you would do and make good on all intentions.

In Catherine's case, she met with James in person and brought along her award-winning butter tarts. James asked her if she wanted to see Sarah, who was in her office. Catherine said, "I appreciate the offer but I came to say hello to you. I will reach Sarah another time." Catherine gained a trusted and valued connection that day with Sarah's gatekeeper, James. She also honoured Sarah by not unexpectedly interrupting her day.

Record your efforts in the Grow Who You Know™ tool:

Final Call

One week later ...

"Oh hi James! It is Catherine Brownlee again and I promise that this is the last time you will hear from me! Oh, I am so glad that you enjoyed the butter tarts; that makes my heart warm, thank you for letting me know! Yes, I would love to chat with Sarah if that is possible."

At this stage in the process, Catherine has made a new friend in James. He will likely extend every effort to ensure that, if Sarah is in the office, she will take the call. If she is not, then one last message will be left on her voicemail.

STEP FIVE:

When you finally make the connection, be 'dressed for success,' with research notes ready and your online calendar open. Catherine recommends standing up for a call such as this, with all other background noises minimized and phone notifications turned off.

1. If you get Sarah directly, start the conversation with the high regard your mom has for her, mention her career and philanthropic history and that you would like to learn more. Set a meeting date and time. If you are meeting in her office, ask what she would like for her favourite beverage.

2. Send the calendar invite to Sarah with the exact time committed to. Include her full name and company, reason for the meeting and location.

Also add phone numbers that may be used in the event of an emergency or if the meeting is delayed in any way. Make it easy for Sarah.

3. If you get voicemail: "Hi Sarah, this is Catherine Brownlee again. I don't want to be a pest and this will be the last time that I call. I just wanted to let you know that I think your success is impressive and, in the future, I would love to learn more. James, your receptionist, is a class act by the way. If there is anything I can do for you, do let me know. Wishing you continued success and, by the way, Mom says 'Hi.' Have the best day!"

When is enough, enough? We recommend you try reaching an individual three times as shown in the examples above.

If you haven't been able to connect in person, leave a phone or email message saying you understand they are very busy and you will not contact them again, although you would enjoy meeting with them in the future should their calendar open up. It is important to provide this closure so your communication is not left dangling.

STEP SIX:

When you are successful in arranging a meeting with the referral, be organized.

- **Have all your research** information contained neatly inside a file folder, labeled with their name and ready for reference
- **Bring the beverage** or treat you promised
- **Have a list of questions** handy. Remember you may only have 10 minutes
- **Set your timer** or keep an eye on your watch to keep track. At the nine-minute mark, thank them for the meeting and say that you see your time is up. In most cases, there is more time in their calendar to continue the meeting and let them decide if they wish to do so

Here are some examples of what you might ask:

- What would you say has been the highlight of your career?
- Who are the thought leaders or mentors who have influenced your success?
- What does success look like for you in the next year?
- How have your philanthropic efforts influenced you?
- What have you looked for in an organization when you have made a career move?

You will know when it is time to talk about you when you are asked. When that happens, ensure your answer is two minutes or less. Then be ready with your next question to turn the conversation back to focus on them.

Take notes during the meeting to keep for future reference.

STEP SEVEN:

After the meeting:

- **Add your notes** in your Grow Who You Know™ tool
- **Send a note of thanks** to them for their time, capturing some of the highlights of your discussion, and reiterating that you are available to serve and support them in the world of work or philanthropy
- **Keep them top of mind** by sending them articles or videos that they may find of interest. **Six times, six different ways, over 6 months (6x6x6™)**

You are now building a foundation of trust, respect and integrity with the goal of moving your new contact to your Love Army™ list.

FINAL STEP:

Always go back to water the well. **Remember to thank the person who gave you the initial referral.** They will almost always start thinking of others they can refer you to. Your Love Army™ wants to be there for you and you need to make it easy for them.

Cat's Tale

From time to time, this process will not work ... at least, initially.

When I joined Canadian Fracmaster as a Technical Sales Representative, I was given a few client files where the relationship with Fracmaster was not very good – or worse – we were told that we would 'never work with them again' for something that happened in the past. The latter was the case with one of the larger energy companies and I was told that we would never 'get them back.' I started following the steps of the Grow Who You Know™ process and, after the third contact, I had made friends with Judith (the receptionist). However, I could not get through to the decision maker.

Six months later I was at a holiday event and I saw him across the room. I approached him and introduced myself and the first thing he said was, "I am so sorry; I forgot to return your call!" As you can imagine, it was most important to seize the moment. I asked him if we could have lunch in the next few weeks and he said, 'Next Tuesday works well for me.' We never looked back. After rebuilding the relationship, our company had another chance and we delivered.

NOTES

ACING THE INTERVIEW

"Practice does not make perfect.
Only perfect practice makes perfect."
Vince Lombardi

YOU GOT THE CALL!

Congratulations! You received a call from either the organization or search firm. The client wants to interview you. If it feels like you've won the lottery, in essence, you have! Your successful application was chosen and qualifies you for the next round closer to the jackpot — your dream job! Now that you have been granted the interview, you have a lot of preparation to do. Let's get going!

PRIVACY AND DIFFICULT QUESTIONS

It is no longer legal for interviewers to ask personal and private questions of interviewees. Capitalizing on your age can be a real benefit: with age comes experience, accomplishments and many examples of how you managed these situations, both good and bad. Also, your level of maturity and ability to make hard decisions will be a great asset to most employers.

Prepare yourself for some of the challenging questions older applicants may be asked regarding salary and why you may not be applying for a management role at this stage in life and career.

There is never any value in trying to act like younger competitors for the role as this will not gain you any points on fitting into the office culture better. In fact, if most of the competitors are quite young, it may not be an ideal environment for you at this stage in your career.

RESEARCH

Find out all you can about the organization from their online web page, from others you know who either may currently work at the company or have worked there, and acquaintances and friends who may have some knowledge to share.

If this is a public company, you can find their annual reports online or request them by mail. Not-for-profit organizations have the option of publishing theirs, or keeping them private, depending on their business model and directors. All registered charities' activities are transparent to the public.

Here is a list of things that will help you prepare for your interview:

Research the company's history, vision and objectives so that you are able to answer questions on them. Research their future plans so you can align their goals with your own job role (and objectives) and detail how you can benefit them in the long run. (www. jobbuzz.com)

Company culture. Is the company filled with conservative folk or creative thinkers? Who are their clients and do your credentials, expertise and personality match their style?

Job description. If you did not receive a detailed job description before applying for the position, you should be able to obtain one from your search firm or directly from the company's human resources department. It's important that you understand the company's description of the role you will fulfill. By having access to that document, it will allow you to formulate the questions you want to ask during the interview.

Find out if the role you are applying for is confidential. If, by chance, you know anyone who works there, this is a great time to take him for coffee.

GETTING READY FOR THE INTERVIEW

Your first impression will be powerful and could be the make-or-break moment. Choose your outfit carefully! Do your research on the company and then dress similarly – and just a little bit better. What you choose will depend again on the culture of the company, the style of office, and the type of work and location. Ask those sources within your reach to provide you with some advice. Under no circumstance should you wear jeans to an interview. Avoiding distractions will ensure the interviewer focuses on your skills and abilities rather than your outfit and accessories. Remember what you wore to the first interview and wear something different to the second one.

Wardrobe choice. Up until now, they have yet to meet you in person. You have been represented by your documents, and perhaps high recommendation from your representing search firm. It is safe to say the hiring company has already viewed your social media sites (we talked about the importance of having a professional head shot in our social media chapter and having your profile content professional and applicable to your career).

Men should avoid white socks. Shoes should complement the attire chosen, and be polished and darker than the rest of the outfit.

Hair, Accessories, Makeup. Both men and women should wear minimal jewelry and remove any facial piercings. If you require glasses, be sure to have the frames updated: do not wear sunglasses. If you have long hair, tie it back or pull it away from your face. Women, make sure your makeup is conservative and your nail polish is not chipped.

We recommend a polish that is either clear, a light colour or French manicured.

We are not suggesting that you will not get the job if you wear red nails, heavy makeup and piercings on your tongue.

Most employers here prefer to interview candidates who are conservative and professional in their approach. Avoiding distractions will ensure the interviewer focuses on your skills and abilities rather than your outfit and accessories.

Get solid sleep. Most of us require six to eight hours of sleep to be at our topmost levels of performance. Interviews add stress to our regular regime and thus require us to accomplish that many hours at minimum. Take measures to sanction your required amount of sleep leading into the day of your interview.

Travelling to an interview. If travel is involved, you'll need to be extra organized. Jet lag and exhaustion from travel can have negative effects on your performance. It is recommended you do not wear your interview clothes if they are at risk of getting wrinkled or stained by a meal enroute to the meeting. Going in advance also allows you to get oriented with the area. Hopefully, you'll have time to do a trial run to the location to ensure your timely arrival will not be affected by heavy traffic or transit systems.

Visualize your success! Prior to your interview, imagine maintaining your usual levels of confidence, intelligence and sharp wit. See yourself working through any awkward scenarios with humour and assuredness.

Cat's Tip

Smile! Smiling releases endorphins, which send messages to your brain that you are happy, content, confident and ready for the next question or scenario.

MIRRORING

Mirroring is the behaviour in which one person subconsciously imitates the gesture, speech pattern, or attitude of another. Mirroring often occurs in social situations and positively affects others' notions about the person who is mirroring them. This will lead to building rapport with others.

TYPES OF INTERVIEWS

Knowing the interview style (or type) will help you prepare mentally, as well as help you determine the list of questions you will prepare. You may be required to do a series of interviews, including some listed here, as well as attend social events:

A telephone interview is almost always the first stage of the interview process. Although we cannot always be prepared when the call comes in, we can do some preliminaries to increase the success of getting past the telephone interview:

- If you are out in public when the call comes in, inform the caller, and ask if it is possible to relocate to a private quieter location within an agreed upon timeframe
- Have all your data ready; this includes some strategic questions to ask the caller
- Stand during the phone call to ensure a tall frame and better voice function
- Smile - energy is invisible and a smile can be perceived over the phone

Panel interviews are common in larger organizations where you may be interviewed by a large or small team. Depending on the size of the company, panel interviews include the person you will be reporting directly to, a member of human resources, and perhaps a senior member of the organization.

Lunch interviews may sound more casual, but are often much more stressful than the other types. Here a fewer key pointers to make the lunch interview successful:

- Turn off your cell phone

- Do not order alcohol

- Stand and greet the interviewer with a web-to-web handshake

- Allow your interviewer to order first and take cue to order a similar item, both for preparation time as well as cost

- Do not order a coffee, tea or dessert after the meal if the interviewer does not

Cat's Tip

Have you ever wondered which bread plate or water glass is yours at a formal dinner place setting? Your worries are over if you can remember "BMW"!
From left to right: "Bread" "Meal" "Water" … it's that easy.

Behavioural Descriptive Interviews (BDI) typically include questions that examine your responses to past challenges, as well as how you'll manage a hypothetical or future situation should you be chosen for the job.

Be prepared to answer questions that relate to successes and failures in both your personal and professional realms. In "Chapter 2: Prepping for Breakthrough," we discussed creating a list of PAR stories that illustrate your successes. We recommended you create a title for each that will trigger your memory during a behavioural interview and can be told in less than a minute. These PAR (Problem-Action-Result) stories will exemplify your past experiences and underscore your capacities to achieve new successes in a future role.

Examples of BDI questions:

Leadership:

"Give me a specific example of something you did that helped build enthusiasm in others."

Stress management:

"Tell me about a difficult situation when it was desirable for you to keep a positive attitude. What did you do?"

Decision making:

"Give me an example of a time you had to make an important or difficult decision. How did you make the decision? How does it affect you today?"

Time management:

"Tell me about a time you had to handle multiple responsibilities. How did you organize the work you needed to do?"

Troubleshooting:

"Give us an example of when you had to deal with a particular (technical, personnel, client, supervisor) problem and how you handled it."

Decision-making:

"Describe a time when you had to subvert a company policy or procedure, or make an important decision on your own, and why you did what you did."

Goal setting:

"Give an example of a goal you reached and tell us how you achieved it."

Team leadership:

"Have you had to convince a team to work on a project they weren't thrilled about? How did you do it?"

In addition to specific examples, you may also be asked to give a general example of a particular success or failure in your personal or occupational life, why you regard this incident as such, and what experience you gained from it.

Remember that every one of your responses may generate five to six additional interviewer questions. For example: Who was involved? What changes ensued? How did that impact your career path? Be as thorough as possible in your PAR story preparation and rehearse your stories out loud. This way, you will be ready for anything.

LINE UP YOUR SUCCESS STORIES

Try to anticipate possible questions and rehearse your answers. Start by studying the job description or posting. What skills is the company looking for?

Listing strengths: Typically, these might include organizational abilities, problem solving, working well under stress, administrative/supervisory capabilities, attention to detail, enjoyment of certain tasks, etc. This is where your success stories are valuable. Having your success stories prepared and ready can give you the confidence that moves an interview from humdrum to outstanding.

Coming up with success stories is one of the most onerous tasks in job search: we are taught that it is poor manners to brag about ourselves. Sharing success stories is not bragging. Quite the opposite! You do not need to state, "I am an incredible salesperson," or "I am an extraordinary leader." Instead, you let the success story say it for you. "I was awarded Top Salesperson three years in a row at Xerox," or "Two of my five-person team won top performer awards and two were promoted to senior positions."

Sharing success stories allows you to articulate your strengths with specific measured results.

Cat's Tool

Have your success stories ready to recite. These are quick and effective stories that underscore your strengths and both qualify and quantify you are the right candidate for the position:

Your story will be less than two minutes and contains three key elements:

1.   Problem (or situation)

2.   Action

3.   Result

You can use the acronym "PAR" to remember these elements. Each should align with the following portion of time:

P   20%

A   60%

R   20%

It's all in the telling: When answering an interview question like, "Describe a decision you made that was unpopular and how you handled its implementation," it is human nature to focus on the problem. But which is more important, the problem itself or the solution you came up with to remedy the problem? When giving your examples in the form of PAR stories, be sure to concentrate most of your time on the actions you took.

The more specific the better: the whole point of Behavioural (Descriptive) Interviewing is to force you to be specific. It gives you a chance to provide examples of when you completed a project, on time and under budget, or how your team achieved its goals despite demanding pressure and limited resources.

If you are a leader, it is your chance to speak out about how someone you mentored went on to do great things, or how, from your team of 12, three were promoted to executive positions within one year.

Your examples will come alive if you use specific dates and names.

Jogging your story recall when under fire: You are probably thinking, "How will I ever remember my stories when being grilled by interviewers?"

Cat's Tip

Give each of your stories a title. The title will be meaningful to you only and will not be shared during the interview. Instead, titling is a great way of helping you categorize each story in your mind so when you are asked to provide examples of "A time when ...," you can easily call up your most appropriate story. For example, when you scan your cheat sheet in the interview and see your title, "I'm OK, You're OK," you will instantly recall your story about helping a client solve a problem. We recommend you come up with between 25-30 stories. Bring your list of titles to the interview for reference.

> Open each PAR story by stating when the situation occurred. "In the third quarter... in the spring of 2005... last March." Likewise, if telling a story about a work associate or manager, use their first name. This helps to ground your response and make it seem plausible.

Another term for behavioural interviews is "Target Selection Interviewing." The objective here is based on discovering how the candidate acts in specific employment-related situations. The logic is that how you behaved in the past will predict how you will behave in the future. This type of interviewing requires you to be confident and on your toes. The best way to achieve this is with practice.

ANSWERING THOSE TOUGH QUESTIONS

There are a few tough questions worth specifically preparing for so they don't become a noose you hang yourself with:

"Tell me about yourself."

The best way to answer this question is to use your "pitch," maybe adding something about education and a more thorough summary plus one interest, hobby or sport you enjoy.

Interviewers don't want to know about your early years on the farm in a dysfunctional family. Honestly.

"Why did you leave?"

Be honest in your response to the inevitable question of why you are looking for a new job (e.g. career ceiling in present position, opportunities for personal growth and advancement, etc.). **Avoid purely monetary considerations** unless you are applying for a commissioned sales position. And never, never denigrate your current or past positions or bosses.

"What is your greatest weakness?"

Almost every interview includes this question, or a version of it.

There are two strategies for answering this question.

The first strategy is to tell the interviewer about a weakness that is really a strength.

For example: "I am a perfectionist. I take care of all the details in each task I perform. The downside is that I work long hours to achieve results and sometimes get too involved in too many projects. I've learned a lot about delegating these past few years. Finding the positive in other people's efforts has helped me let go of perfection."

OR

"I have a hard time saying no. When people ask me to do something, I typically say yes and then work overtime to get it all done. I've been working on this specifically, and I feel I have learned to share my priorities with the people on my team and engage them in delegating tasks."

Your second strategy is to choose a weakness that you have overcome.

For example: "I was very shy and hated public speaking. I decided to overcome my fear so I joined Toastmasters and took a public speaking course through continuing education. Last year I was the emcee at my cousin's wedding, in front of 200 guests! And my past company sent me to an investor-relations meeting where I presented our department's results."

"My natural personality type is disorganized. I have taken four courses on time management through Mount Royal College and U of C and have read numerous books on the topic. On my last performance review, my manager praised my organization not only in my workspace but in the way I complete projects. I have a copy of the review here if you would like to see it."

Weakness tips:

Do not brush over this question with a glib response. Provide an honest answer, using a true weakness and providing examples to support it.

Review your weakness with your references to make sure they would agree. Coach them on how you plan to respond to this question so you are in alignment.

Don't discuss more than one weakness and never choose one that will directly affect the position.

Be willing to be vulnerable. It is disarming to hear a person's true weakness and will draw the interviewer closer to you.

Have specific examples of how you've overcome the weakness and what the results have been.

"Who do you admire?" or "What book are you reading?"

Interviewers will sometimes ask you to discuss someone you admire or what book you are reading. These questions help to round out their perspective of your interests and values. It's best to have thought these through in advance. A good choice of someone you admire is always someone who has had a positive influence on your life.

Your book choice can be as varied as a library's bookshelves. If you are reading a current, well-known author or article, this might get the interviewer's attention.

The topic of money:

Be prepared for a question or two about your current salary or total compensation package. The verdict is still out on how you should respond. Many recruiters and hirers suggest this question must be specifically answered before a second meeting can be set. Others believe that candidates have the right to not divulge their current salary.

If queried in your first interview about your monetary expectations, try not to give specific dollar or range figures. You could handle this question by stating that, while remuneration is important, you are primarily interested in this opportunity. Then give several reasons why you are seeking this particular position with this particular company (even if you have stated this earlier in the interview). If pushed further, mention your current salary range, and add that **you would expect to be reimbursed commensurate with your qualifications, background and experience and the existing marketplace for such skills.**

Casual Questions:

Some interviewers will ask questions that may be quite tricky as a means of getting to know your personality, such as "Are you a dog or a cat person?" It will be important to just be yourself and have fun in answering them.

AVOIDING THE NERVOUS BREAKDOWN

Being well prepared will definitely help you with nerves, as will practice. Try to have as many meetings as possible leading up to an interview so that the give and take of information sharing becomes comfortable. Even interviewers are nervous until they have had plenty of experience.

It's true being interviewed can still make you break into a cold sweat. A great way to combat nerves is to tell the interviewer right off the bat, "This is my first interview in 15 years and I'm nervous." Saying it out loud will dissipate some of the stress.

One man we worked with experienced close to a panic attack each time he was interviewed. We coached him to bring his fear into the open. At his next interview, he introduced himself by saying, "How I interview is not a reflection on how I work. I find interviewing extremely stressful since I'm introverted and like to focus on my work." He stumbled through the interview, highlighting his accomplishments through PAR stories and got the job.

INTERVIEW DAY

An interview can seem to have an unequal balance of power. After all, interviewers have the authority to hire or reject you. You can choose to feel inferior. But there is another way to look at the interview situation that will make you more comfortable with the process.

Think of it as dating: you and the interviewer are both trying to decide who would be the best mate. Remember, you are two (or more) adults trying to determine if your joining the company is a fit. If they don't hire you, they are doing you a favour, because they have determined you won't be happy and/or productive inside their company. Similarly, you need to decide before accepting their offer if the company culture is the right place for you. It is much easier to decline before taking the job than after you have made a definite commitment.

PRACTICE MENTAL IMAGERY

Before the interview, and as far ahead as possible, start imagining how the interview will go. Here is where those laws of attraction return. This mental imagery practice can have amazing results. Not only will you feel more confident, your connections with the interviewer can be stronger.

Imagine how you will be received. Visualize a positive exchange and great conversation that allows you to really connect with your interviewers.

Interviewers are real people, just like you. They might have had a recent fight with their spouse, or their teenager is acting out, or their dog just passed away. Imagine you are being interviewed by a future friend who is genuinely interested in knowing all about you and is open to sharing about the company and team.

Try it. You have nothing to lose and everything to gain.

WAITING IN THE LION'S DEN

Turn OFF your cell phone

We know, we know. We shouldn't have to mention this, but you would be astonished by how many people forget to turn their cell phone off before they enter the interview. By then it is too late. It is rude and annoying when the ring tone is left on and interrupts the meeting.

Breathe

Be sure to arrive 10 minutes early so you are relaxed and have a chance to acclimatize yourself and check out the surroundings.

To calm yourself, you simply need to breathe. People who suffer from panic attacks and anxiety can turn their symptoms around merely by breathing. The proper technique is to breathe in slowly through your nose deep into your diaphragm, count your breaths and then try to exhale for longer than you inhale. When people are afraid, they tend to breathe shallowly, which sets off the whole flight or fight syndrome. Once the body experiences shallow breathing it will begin to tremble, shake, the heart rate accelerates, and vision becomes blurred and tunnel like – all not good for making an ideal impression.

If you have a few minutes to sit in the waiting area, push both your feet firmly into the ground and breathe. You will find yourself much more relaxed.

The same rule applies if you get nervous during the interview. Don't hesitate to stop and take a deep breath.

Get the lay of the land

In the unlikely event that you haven't done your homework prior to arriving at the interview, you can glean important information while you're waiting.

If there is a receptionist, chat with him or her. Get to know them in a genuine way. Be interested. Lots of hiring managers will ask the receptionist about his or her impression of the candidate.

If the company's annual report or a recent promotional article is resting on the coffee table, take a minute to skim the highlights. Some companies even have their mission statement mounted on a plaque.

The waiting period between your arrival and the interview itself provides you a chance to come up with an icebreaker.

What to take

Bring a leather portfolio with the following items:

- Your personalized business cards
- The nicest pen you own
- Blank paper for note-taking
- At least three copies of your résumé and references. The interviewer(s) may not have a copy of your documents. Some interviewers will test you to see how organized you are.
- A list of references, presented at the end of the first interview, illustrating the level of confidence in your suitability for that perfect position. You may want to refer to your résumé as well during the interview, to ensure the accuracy of dates, so bring a copy for yourself.
- Copies of your performance evaluations, awards, and letters of reference, neatly copied and stapled in case your interviewer(s) request copies. These should provide backup for points stated in your résumé.
- Your cheat sheet, which will include your list of questions, plus the titles of your 25 to 30 success stories in the following categories:
    - Job related
    - Getting along with others
    - Time demands
    - Special to your area of expertise

If you know the names of your interviewer(s) in advance (which we highly recommend you take the time to find out), you will want to have written their names and titles on a piece of paper or have their printed LinkedIn profile or Executive profile from their website. This will help you to remember who's who and will allow you to more easily respond to interviewers by their first name throughout the interview.

First impressions are everything. There is great debate over whether or not the decision to hire is made during the first three minutes of meeting. If this is true, then you need to make the most of this time.

HANDSHAKE

Your handshake, too, can convey so much about you. A weak, limp, dead-fish handshake can make you appear cold and lacking in enthusiasm. A hand-crushing shake can leave an equally poor impression, as can grabbing the interviewer's hand with both of yours and then pumping frantically.

If you're out of practice, be sure to rehearse a firm-gripped, vertical handshake in the days leading up to the interview.

Be polite. Have a smile ready for everyone – and we mean everyone, from the receptionist to the other staff members you come across on the way to the place of interview. You never know, you may be working with them in the future. The same is true if you are being interviewed with other people. You might also end up working alongside them.

Be authentic. You have often heard the advice about always being true to yourself. It is normal during an interview to show your best side. This is the point: you show your best side, not pretend to be something or someone that you are not. If you are true to yourself and express your true personality, you will come across as natural and real during the interview. You will be able to deliver more truthful answers, and the interviewers will also be able to sense that.

Be confident. Remove and resist any negative energy you may be feeling or carrying as it is reflected to all around you. Your greatest strength in an interview is your own intuition. You may be expressing that all is well, but if you've attached yourself to a negative vibe, it will be the most obvious thing you portray. You won't likely be invited to a second interview.

No matter how nervous you are, always look confident. Nobody wants to hire a person who is nervous during the interview, as it creates an impression that the candidate may be unable to handle workplace situations.

HERE'S LOOKING AT YOU

Of all the ways we communicate with people, eye contact is one of the most powerful. People judge sincerity, honesty and confidence through eye contact.

If you are particularly shy and it feels uncomfortable to look directly into the interviewer's eyes, then gaze generally at the eyebrow area or the bridge of the nose. It can also help if you let your vision go slightly out of focus.

We're not suggesting you stare unblinkingly at the interviewer through a 45-minute interview. Research shows a gaze that lasts longer than seven to 10 seconds can cause discomfort or anxiety. It's certainly appropriate to look away as you collect your thoughts or prepare for each of your answers. When you first meet the interviewer, and then throughout the interview, you need to show with your eyes that you are both sincere and interested.

Cat's Tip

Get business cards or jot down interviewer(s) names

In the unlikely event that you didn't find out the interviewers' names and titles prior to the interview, wait until you have been seated and introduced to everyone, and then ask if you could have one of their business cards.

If cards are unavailable, jot down their names on the blank paper from your portfolio and ensure you have the proper spelling. (This will come in handy as you refer to the interviewers by name throughout the interview and when you write your thank you letters after the interview.)

BODY LANGUAGE

Body language carries significant weight during interviews. Do not slouch. Slouching makes you come across as someone who is lazy and sometimes maybe even sick. On the other hand, standing or sitting ramrod-straight may make you appear stiff and unyielding unless, of course, you are a candidate for a position in the military ranks.

If you have mannerisms such as bouncing your knee, tapping your foot on the floor or your fingers on top of the table, or wringing your hands, try to correct them. These are often signs of being nervous, and you do not want your prospective employers to think you are terrified of them.

PREPARE AN OPENER

Your plan when you meet the interviewer is to stand straight and make good eye contact as you shake his or her hand, or several hands – firmly. But what should you be saying while everyone gets settled?

A good interviewer will put you at ease by talking about your interests or something pleasant on your résumé. The problem is that there are too few good interviewers, and those who are may have had little time to prepare.

How about something more meaningful? "I'm so glad you had the time to meet with me, especially since you must be so busy with the Stampede expansion right now ... or since it is budget season right now ... or as the gas price is so low, or as you must be busy figuring out different strategies ... or coaching women's hockey."

ADDITIONAL TIPS:

Clarify

When the interviewer asks you a question, make sure you understand what is being asked. You have every right to ask for clarification if you are not sure. When in doubt, paraphrase what you thought they said.

Pause, respond, get specific

Once you've heard the question, take a little pause to think before answering. Refer to your cheat sheet of PAR story titles to find the one most appropriate to the question. You only need one example for each question.

You are looking for an example with a result. Each answer to a question will involve one story or example. Remember back in grade school when the English teacher said that each sentence is one idea? The same rule applies to your interview responses. Think of each example as an expansion of one bullet from your résumé.

If you blank out

Don't panic. This can happen to anyone. If you go completely blank, state that you are having trouble thinking of an answer. Ask the interviewer if it is all right for you to get back to the question later and then write it down on your paper. You must take responsibility for bringing the question up again before the end of the interview.

Stay honest

One plant manager we worked with said that he had people interviewed three times by three different people and that the answers were later compared to see if there were any discrepancies. Your best bet is to be honest. When recruiters are interviewing and get the feeling the respondent is not being honest, they can be like dogs on a bone, asking and asking until they get the truth. Not a pleasant experience.

Be yourself

You may get the feeling in an interview that you are encased in ice or that you've suddenly become a robot. The whole interview process seems a bit bizarre. Here you are expected to make a decision about joining a company after one or more meetings. Imagine if marriages were arranged that quickly.

The interviewer wants to know if you have the qualifications they are looking for and if you fit. Even though it is a contrived situation, do everything you can to let your true self shine through. Crack a joke if that is what you usually do; talk about an interest you're passionate about. Let them know who you really are so you can both decide if this is truly the right fit.

Avoid the negative

If you speak negatively during the interview, the interviewers will see you as a negative person. Keep your responses positive. If you have to talk about a problem, keep your description fewer than six words... "I was let go due to restructuring."

One of the greatest errors people make in interviews is to talk for too long about the problem. Remember to keep the problem under six words. The action and result are the bulk of what you want to talk about.

If the interviewer becomes a zombie

If you are responding to a question and the interviewer is staring into space with that deer-in-the-headlights expression and probably thinking, "Milk, eggs, bread, then I'll fill up with gas ... I wonder if I'll have time to go to the drycleaners ... Mary looked a little under the weather," stop talking! Ask them the magic interview phrase; "Was that enough information?" Nine out of 10 times, they will say, "Yes it is." And you can move on.

Get feedback

Don't be afraid to ask for feedback at any stage of the interview. When providing your own examples, you might ask if a similar situation has arisen within their company and if your solution would be applicable. This gives you the opportunity to identify and address major concerns that the company has. Maintain the attitude that all problems can be resolved and that you are quite serious in your expectations.

Ask insightful questions. At some point during the interview, the interviewer or staff asking the questions, may turn the tables and let you ask questions. It is possible that you have a lot of questions running through your head about the job. Go through these questions mentally and ask only the insightful ones, or those that make sense.

Interviewers tend to remember the candidates who posed challenging questions to them. Usually, interviewees ask how much the job will pay them on a monthly or annual basis. They may even inquire about vacation time and other benefits. This is a natural curiosity for the candidate but, depending on the execution, or the way the question was asked, it may make you look like your sole interest in the job is the compensation or vacation time offered.

Be sure to have a list of 10 good interview questions to ask about the job and the company. Have the questions written out in a notepad and have a pen ready to take notes.

Suggestions on some interviewing questions for you to ask:

- What are the expectations of the first 90 days in this position?
- What are some of the projects this position will work on?
- Who does this person report to? Straight line or dotted line reporting?
- What type of training will this position receive?
- How will this position be measured on success?
- Very last question to ask is: "Based on the information you have received about me today, do you have any concerns that would prevent you from hiring me for this job?"

Match the communication style of the interviewer. You have to connect with them, while making sure your personality is showing. You can do this by mirroring his or her manner. Be business-like when he or she is business-like. Try to be more personable or adapt a casual tack when you see that they are going that way. If they ask direct questions, then you should supply direct answers.

Wrapping it up

There are a few things you must determine before the interview is terminated.

First, **ask for feedback.** Doing so portrays a positive impression of your keenness towards the job. Don't be afraid to ask for feedback at any stage of the interview. As the interview is about to close, ask the interviewer how the interview went and your suitability for their team and your potential place within it. Ask if they have any particular concerns; this will be your final chance to deal with any problems.

Second, **ask about the next step** in the selection process. It is perfectly appropriate to ask how many candidates are being interviewed for the position. Show interest in the process and in the company.

Third, **ask if there is anyone else they would like you to meet** right away. In a final interview situation, you may ask if it is possible to meet with other members of the company.

If time allows, request a tour of the workplace. Companies often prefer eager candidates to those who are better qualified, but indifferent.

Acknowledge clearly what they perceived as the shortcoming and then address, with examples from your past, why that is not a roadblock at all.

So many times people say, "I can't believe I forgot to tell them about this or that." Look on the bright side. You have something fresh to put into your thank you letter. Don't say you forgot to mention a particular strength or experience. Instead, just state that you wanted to highlight that you ... and give the PAR story.

WHAT NOT TO DO IN AN INTERVIEW

If there are DOs in participating in job interviews as the interviewee, there are also DON'Ts, or things that you must avoid doing, because they are likely to ruin your chances of landing the job.

Do not speak ill of past employers. Expect interviewers to ask several questions about your work history, particularly on your past employment. They might even bait you when they start asking the reasons why you quit or were separated from the company. Do not badmouth your previous employers, not even if they were the employers from hell and your complaints are completely valid. You should always talk about them positively, but do not go to the extent of making up stories just to make them look good. In the same manner, do not offer information about your previous companies, because this is a sign of disloyalty. The interviewer will conclude that, if you can to do it with your previous employers, you may do it with them in future.

Do not talk too much. Talking too much, or taking too long in providing answers for direct questions will give your interviewers the impression that you have trouble getting to the point. This could also mean that you are just bluffing because you don't know a thing about what you are saying.

Do not display impatience. Is the interview running late? Just stay calm and cool, and wait patiently. This may actually be done on purpose, to see how patient you are. Constantly looking at your watch or having your impatience show on your face will certainly not earn you any points.

Interviewing for a job is one of the crucial steps in getting hired. If you consider yourself to be a poor interviewee, make an effort to change this. You can never really do away with interviews, because all job hiring and recruitment processes conduct them. Even a simple conversation with the employer may count as an interview.

POST-INTERVIEW

After an interview, always keep your activity level high

We have a superstition about keeping the activity level high. The more energy you have going, the more energy you will attract.

Once you've had that great interview, there is a tendency to want to rest on your laurels and wait by the phone like a lovesick high school student. And you will also be less disappointed if you don't get the phone call because other fabulous activities are in the works.

Now is when you need to get three completely new activities started. Meet a new contact, take a course, research a new company and send a letter.

In the event that you are not hired

If the interview went well and for some crazy reason you are not hired, try not to be too disheartened.

Allow the interviewer to enter the circle of people who love you.

Feel free to ask for an information interview, from which you might gain insight, referrals and advice. Request this interview within the next six weeks, explaining that you would like to include them as a networking resource. Then keep the 6x6x6™ rule of keeping in touch with them – "six times over the next six months in six different ways."

If you want to use the person as an information source, avoid asking for interview feedback or a list of reasons why you did not get the job. When a person feels a future meeting is likely to be negative or highly-charged, your chances of continuing the connection decrease.

Follow-up!

As soon as you finish the interview, go and buy a coffee or something stronger. Write down your notes about the interview. Pay attention to any shortcomings they thought you had, anything you forgot to say that was important, and any challenges they are facing that you can think of solutions for. Use your notes to create a tailored thank you letter, which should be sent to all interviewers, the same day if possible.

If you are working with a recruiter and they presented you to the company, then call or email the recruiter after the interview and confirm whether or not you are interested in going to the next level. The recruiter will then have the opportunity to request feedback from their client and pass this information back to you.

Tips for thank you letters after interviews

If you definitely want the job, start your letter off by stating this and expressing appreciation for the interview. In the body of the letter, emphasize the highlights of the interview and the reasons you are a good fit with the company. Feel free to use bullets to highlight the top three reasons why you are the ideal candidate for the job or why you would love the challenge of joining their team.

Here is where you can also address any shortcomings that were raised. Was there something specific they had an issue with?

For example:

"We like you, but you're over qualified." Reiterate that you are at the time of your career where you would love a challenge like they're offering and have no desire for advancement.

"We like you, but we wanted someone more senior." Provide them examples of how quickly you've been promoted in each previous job you've had. Even in high school you ended up managing the bakery you were working at.

"You would need training in SAP to work with us." Go through your PAR stories and find examples of a time you were trained quickly on a new system.

NOTES

CHAPTER NINE

NEGOTIATING THE OFFER

"Wise are those who learn that the bottom line does not always have to be their top priority."
William Arthur Ward

All your hard work and efforts landed you a job offer! This is truly a huge moment in your career and the following chapter will walk you through the processes involved and assist you in making the best decision for you and your new organization.

POWER POSITIONING

Ownership. For the first time in this entire process, the power is yours.

The offer is symbolic that you are exactly what the company needs to advance their objectives; the ball is in your court. Navigate this next step with intelligence, respect and careful timing to create a win/win situation for both you and your new employer.

In the earlier chapter, "Prepping for Breakthrough," we created a chart aimed to help you decide if the opportunity is right for you, even before you apply for the vacancy. This same chart will also be helpful in deciding whether to accept or decline the offer.

Taking a few days to have meaningful discussions with your family or those being directly affected by your decision is very important.

Sorting the facts

Once you've decided to accept the position, gather some acceptable ranges or options should the negotiations require flexibility:

- What is the one thing you must have?
- What are you willing to relinquish to achieve this role?
- What would you like to be different?
- What would you add to this offer?

PRE-NEGOTIATION HOMEWORK

A question we believe is very important in the negotiation process is to ask the recruiter if it is possible to have a 30-minute coffee with an individual who is already in the position. For employers, offering an opportunity for the potential hire to have a conversation with an existing employee already in that position is a great idea for a few reasons:

- They will give authentic responses
- There will be a sense of trust developed
- The responses will be more accurate, as they are coming from someone who is living the experience
- You may realize there is a good sense of fit or not one at all

It is important to not only gain a better understanding of the job that needs to be done and the skills associated with it, but also the people and company culture as well.

STRATEGIES

Once there is an offer on the table

Once the offer is made to you, clarify the details as precisely as possible. What is the company offering you exactly in terms of hours, benefits, responsibilities, compensation, vacation, stock options, etc.? If they haven't already put the specifics in writing, jot down notes during the meeting and have them verify that this is the offer and sign it. Then tell them you need 24 to 48 hours to review the offer. Arrange a time to meet in a couple of days. It is in your favour to have a face-to-face meeting.

Revisit your top three criteria and see how closely the offer fits. Talk the offer over with your significant other or trusted mentors to help you gain perspective.

This is when patience comes into play

If you've been job-hunting for a while, you may want to jump at the first offer, for fear it is the only one. However, we know after years of working with people that receiving one offer indicates more are on the way. Whatever you commit to will be hard to undo once you've accepted the offer, so be sure the terms are acceptable to you.

Your best negotiation tactics

Before returning for the negotiating meeting, organize your thoughts into three categories:

- What you like about the offer
- What you would like to change
- What else you would like to add to the offer

Here are some strategies for conducting the negotiating meeting itself:

Take charge

This is your meeting. You've set the agenda, so be clear about what you want and on what you're willing to bend.

Reiterate the goal

Positively let them know you want to negotiate an offer and are excited about the job. During the process, repeat the goal as many times as necessary.

Stress the win-win

Both parties want the same thing, namely a great match and terms you both can be committed to. State this and remain positive.

Put everything on the table

Say everything you want, item by item. Do not play games or pull out cards later in the process. That will only erode their trust in you. If you liked their salary offer and only want to negotiate vacation time, say that up front. If you need $10,000 more a year, let them know and work together to see where you can come up with it. It could, for example, take the form of a bonus, stock options, or a matched savings plan. The more you work with them, the better it will be for both of you.

Give no personal reasons

You are negotiating in a work place, not with a future spouse. Your personal reasons for wanting these changes are irrelevant and inappropriate to bring up at this time. It is enough that you want these items; you do not need to bring up sick parents, eight children at home, an unemployed spouse, or an expensive chocolate habit.

Think before you speak

In the interviewing process it was appropriate to be forthcoming with information. During negotiation, it is important to think before you speak. Allow time for pauses and let them fill in gaps in the conversation. Remain positive and friendly, but allow yourself time to reflect.

Handle multiple offers gracefully

What if you receive two or more offers at the same time? This is very likely when you follow our recommendations. Do let them know that you are considering other offers. Try not to play them off one another, however. In the short term it may seem to work in your favor, but doing so can easily erode trust with two or more potential employers at this stage. If they ask you the terms being offered by the other company, you may tell them that all offers are confidential, including theirs.

Don't accept until you are ready

You may be ready to accept at this stage. If not, we suggest you request more time to think it over. (The amount of time one takes to consider an offer is also negotiable.) You are making a huge commitment and deserve time to be absolutely sure. You may want to run it past an employment lawyer. Respect their time frame and be reasonable. Be sure both you and the company sign the offer.

You have to know when to fold!

Remember, both you and the employer are striving for a win-win. They want you to have a compensation package and work environment that keeps you committed, especially in a competitive environment. Ask for what you want, keeping your top criteria in mind. When a fair and reasonable offer is made, one that matches what is important to you, then it is time to accept and embrace your new role. If you follow the steps we suggest, we are confident your next great job is just around the corner.

Wrapping things up after you accept an offer

Finally, all your hard work has paid off. Now is the time to wrap up loose ends. Contact each of your references and let them know about your new position. Thank them for their contribution to your success.

It will be important to leave your current position with the best possible attitude. It's standard to give at least two weeks' notice. If your employer wants you to work through your notice period, make sure your office and projects are in order. "Do unto others as you would have them do unto you," should be your motto. In other words, leave things as you'd like to find them if you were the boss or your replacement.

If people ask why you are leaving, it's appropriate to give general statements like, "This is a great opportunity I just can't pass up."

Stay positive. Help in whatever ways you can to make this a smooth transition for everyone. People remember both their first and last impressions of someone, so use this time to your advantage, not your detriment.

RESIGNATION

Starting a new position usually means leaving an old one. Making a smooth transition without leaving scars or burning bridges is sometimes challenging, especially in a competitive market, but it is possible.

Once you've accepted your new role, notify your references and all those who are directly affected by your upcoming departure. It is customary to give two week's notice to your current organization, but this is not always the case. For those in higher and more powerful executive roles, your exodus comes the moment you announce you're moving on. In these cases, a human resources representative is involved, an information technician will likely confiscate all your media devices and your files will be locked.

If you know in advance you will be leaving, it is wise to ensure all the essentials of what is rightfully yours and that of the company have been rectified and specified.

Your resignation letter needs not be long, but it should contain some key points and is typically required for the company's legal records:

- Effective date of resignation
- Explanation for leaving
- A positive accolade for the company or your team
- A promise to ensure minimal disruption

Example:

February 1, 2018

Company and Address

Attention: Russell Clark, Vice President

Dear Russ:

Please accept this letter as my official notice of resignation effective February 19, 2017. I have accepted a position with Shymt Engineering, which provides me with an opportunity to further my career goals in the energy industry.

It has been my pleasure to work with Kaleidoscope Systems these past three years. I have appreciated the friendly environment and the interesting and varied projects our team has worked on from concept to completion. I wish you and Kaleidoscope continued success in the future.

It is my intention to work diligently with you to wrap up as much as possible within the next two weeks. If you have any suggestions on how we can best accomplish that goal, please share your thoughts with me, as I am eager to leave on the most positive note possible.

Thank you.

Respectfully,

Bob Brown

NOTES

CHAPTER TEN

SUCCESSFUL ONBOARDING

"Everybody is a genius. But if you judge a fish by its ability to climb a tree, it will live its whole life believing that it is stupid."

Albert Einstein

Onboarding is the process of helping a new hire adjust effectively and efficiently to social and performance aspects of their new job. Most organizations have their own methodologies for accomplishing these tasks; usually they are a mix of formal and informal ways.

Formal: a scripted set of forms or processes that are a requirement set out by the organization to ensure that each step has been accomplished successfully.

Informal: the employee learns and adjusts to the role without adhering to a checklist or specific format.

According to Society for Human Resource Management (SHRM), research and conventional wisdom both suggest employees have approximately 90 days to prove themselves in a new job. The faster the new hire feels welcome and prepared for their roles, the sooner they contribute to the organizations mission. (www.SHRM.org)

Successful onboarding includes coaching, feedback, follow-up, support, etc., and improves the following aspects:

- Employee contribution
- Individual and group productivity
- Relational trust and networking
- Role transitioning
- Acceptance of the organization and culture

Further, the value of successful onboarding is as follows:

- Improves clarity of role definitions, boundaries and expectations
- Increases job satisfaction
- Enhances job performance
- Reduces turnover

Some tools that can be applied to improve onboarding success include a script or agenda of the timelines for follow-ups, checklists to ensure certain measures have been put in place, or matters and opportunities have been discussed.

One important tool is feedback. This can be as formal as performance appraisals or as informal as a coffee or lunch meeting. However it is performed, the results will lead to continued open lines of communication and an affirmation of objectives for all parties involved.

As a new employee, it is important that you request a timeline for when feedback and performance appraisals will be scheduled. Be prepared to discuss the following during the meeting:

- What is working
- What needs improvement
- Clarification of role, responsibilities and deliverables
- Plan for next steps

FOUR LEVELS OF ONBOARDING

The building blocks of successful onboarding are often called the Four C's.

Compliance includes teaching employees basic legal and policy-related rules and regulations.

Clarification ensures employees understand the expectations of their new role, how their individual contribution leads to and affects the success of the overall organization, and what success looks like in terms of their individual and team performance.

Culture includes providing employees with a sense of organizational norms - both formal and informal. This includes the overarching vision for the organization (why the company exists besides making money), as well as the core values (what is acceptable and what won't be tolerated specific to the organization).

Connection refers to vital interpersonal relationships and information networks that new employees must establish. Of critical importance are the relationships with their direct supervisor(s) and any direct report(s), as well as closest working peers.

The degree to which each organization leverages these four building blocks determines its overall onboarding strategy, with most firms falling into one of three levels:

Passive Onboarding is present in virtually all organizations and firms, where new employees are provided the essentials of how the company expects the new member to behave and introduces him to the culture. Often there are no formal checklists. This is typically an unsystematic process.

High Level Onboarding is when an organization utilizes a formal approach to the firm's practices and expectations. This affects the employee's connection to the organization's culture. This type of onboarding is usually systematic and formal.

Proactive Onboarding aligns with a company that has a human resources management approach to launching the employee's new job within the establishment.

SHORT-TERM BENEFITS OF ONBOARDING

One of the largest and most profound results of successful onboarding is the employee's self-confidence and thus positive job performance. Motivation is high and self-fulfillment translates into results, commitment and the bottom line.

If an employee clearly comprehends his role, negative aspects like role conflict and turf wars are reduced. Support and strong team relationships evolve when each employee knows what they are expected to do within their respective roles.

Socialization within the organization leads to acceptance by colleagues, quicker adjustment and sound communication and trust among all colleagues.

Cat's Tip

New hires can apply some of these tactics to facilitate their own smooth successful onboarding:

- Establish and grow a working relationship with your supervisor by taking on tasks and ensuring they are fully completed, with request for feedback and criticism
- Engage in conversations with your peers, even about mundane topics
- Socialize over breaks and create informal opportunities to have a conversation
- Show initiative in attending voluntary company gatherings or hosted events

Knowing and navigating the firm's mission and values helps a new employee to speak the language and thus establishes a sense of fitting well and feeling satisfied with the choice to work there. In turn, this improves performance, confidence and the opportunity for advancement.

LONG-TERM BENEFITS OF ONBOARDING

Here are some of the most notable long-term results of successfully onboarded personnel:

- Lower turnover
- Increased performance
- High job satisfaction
- Commitment to company and role
- Lower stress levels
- Cost reductions through less frequent management time on training, fewer job placement ads, and any customer turnover associated with key personnel changes (especially if they are customer-facing)

COACHING AND MENTORING

Ideally, the stakeholders, including HR, training staff and mentors are key to the successful onboarding of new hires. When that is not possible, it is recommended the employee engage an external coach to help them become powerful tools for the organization's overall successes.

When an internal coach (or internal supervisor skilled in coaching) is not available, an external coach can be a valuable asset to an organization. Even on a shoestring budget, an external coach can be brought in on an infrequent basis to address key personnel or the entire team.

A great coach can help a single team member or the entire staff with the following:

- Improving motivation
- Creating strategies and tools for successful habits
- Reducing or resolving interpersonal conflict
- Equipping the team to handle stressful situations or difficult customers
- Mapping employee career development and fulfillment
- Developing talent by helping the executive team in placing the right team members into the right roles based on their motivation, skills, and behavioural styles
- Assisting with strategic planning
- Reframing challenging circumstances and ineffective actions
- Identifying hidden potential in employees, economic conditions, and industry trends

In short, hiring the right person is not the finish line. The right employee can become despondent, jaded, and take on a negative, toxic attitude if they are not treated with respect and onboarded well.

Hiring the right person the right way is the real 'finish line' (if there ever is one in business), and the secret here is in effective onboarding.

NOTES

CHAPTER ELEVEN

WHEN IN ROME...

*"If you should be in Rome, live in the Roman manner;
if you should be elsewhere, live as they do there."*

Attributed to Saint Ambrose

LET THE ADVENTURE BEGIN!

As global citizens our employment opportunities are infinite! When planning to advance your career globally, multicultural awareness is critical for your future success both socially and in business. This chapter will examine the nuances of foreign business practices, laws, social trends, plus political and governmental systems.

Are you competing against locals for the same position? Are there any cultural barriers or road blocks, such as language, religious or political stances, or personal safety issues that you should be prepared to handle?

SPONSORSHIPS

If you are being sponsored by an organization that has the experience of moving people around the globe, a foundation will have already been laid for the processes required to complete the transition for expatriates. This will include administrative approvals, legal fees, immigration documents and visas, medical exams, housing, schooling and perhaps even a few perks to sweeten the offer.

While it is healthy to dream big, it is also imperative to be realistic and comprehend the challenges and possible restrictions. Many countries that experience economic devastation, political warfare, terrorist threats or the decline of a national economy are often the very countries that offer to pay incredible salaries to those who are willing to set up camp there to make their fortunes as an expatriate.

Cat's Tool

One of Cat's favourite books on this topic is by **Terri Morrison,** ***Kiss, Bow or Shake Hands*** (McGrawHill, 1994). Since its original publication, many newer editions have been published, as well as subsequent individual editions, focused solely on countries, regions or global areas. There are PDF versions and online portals which also allow access to this handbook. The original handbook has cultural details for 60 different countries.

SOCIAL AND BUSINESS ETIQUETTE

Being prepared and educated for any business engagement is an indicator of respect towards the hosting country and exemplifies your professionalism. This approach to business portrays an earnest desire to do business in accordance with your foreign contacts. In this section, we will explore some of the most important elements required to support you in achieving deeper and more meaningful results and provide you with some handy guidelines.

BEFORE YOU GO

Do some basic research on the country and area you will be visiting. While some customs and social behaviours are somewhat generalized between country borders, there are often subtle (and not-so-subtle) regional differences.

Cat's Tip

Use this as a resource tool to educate yourself prior to travelling for business to any country:

In the Google search bar type "Business Etiquette (country)"

Place the name of the country you will be visiting inside the brackets above.

Below are some rules of thumb that will help you sort the types of information you will need to know when attending events, meeting locals and feeling comfortable with different social and business cultures.

NATIONAL HISTORY: Learn the basics about the country you will spend time in.

Government:

> Learn about the hosting country's history and perhaps how it was established. Understanding these influencing factors can often aid in being a better guest as well as a more compassionate listener – an essential skill in business.

Language:

> Even if you aren't fluent in the host country's language, it's always beneficial to learn some of the basics. Locals appreciate a foreigner who is trying to establish a common ground of communication. Asking for lingual guidance is also a great way to start new conversations.

Religious influences:

> This is a broad area, but generally speaking, be aware of any hotspots. Making light of a historical event to create humour, may only be humourous from your own perspective, especially if the historical event affected that country in a negative way.

Demographics:

> Understand how the country is influenced by its geography, natural resources and economic influences and restrictions.

CULTURAL ORIENTATION: Discover how this country thinks and does things differently.

Ways of thinking:

> Typically, we align our own methods of thinking and behaving based on what we know and do naturally. So do residents of other countries. These differences carry the potential to cause awkwardness or conflict. Be open-minded, non-judgmental and intentionally curious.

BUSINESS PRACTICES: This is not a time to guess; the risks could be too high.

Negotiations:

Negotiations, or final decisions, are typically completed via three key factors: faith, fact and feeling. Each of these elements have numerous and complicate layers. Recommendations will be made in accordance with priority, such as what's best for the corporation, or within the constraints of the legal system, or even whether it's ethically sound.

Finding the right balance between knowing when to listen, contribute respectfully and draw upon your instinct are keys to successful business arrangements. When uncertain, take the time to do research on the issue or consult an expert in the field before making an educated decision.

Etiquette:

With so much information available to us, it's easy to quickly learn the appropriate etiquette and behaviour when communicating with foreigners. Such elements as attire, where and when to conduct business, appropriate eye contact and use of names, can be critical factors when you're being considered as a business prospect.

Cat's Tool

Expatriate Forums:

Moving to Canada:

www.expatexchange.com/canada/liveincanada.html

Moving out of Canada:

www.expatforum.com

www.transitionsabroad.com

Compare the cost of living costs between countries:

www.Expatistan.com

Cat's Tale

We wrote a bestseller, Want to Work in Oil and Gas?, in 2007 promoting career success in the then booming oil and gas industry in Calgary. I was invited to attend and promote this book at the very first O&G show in India. Two weeks prior to departing, I received some strong recommendations from good friends not to adhere to my usual spontaneous approach to travel abroad. At least not to India.

To make hotel arrangements, I contracted an agent, who informed me that the Diwali was occurring at the same time as the O&G show: there was zero vacancy. Luckily, my Calgary friends had family in New Delhi and sought their support on my behalf. In spite of their local efforts, not even a rental flat or guesthouse could be found for me, until just three days before my flight. All I was told was that someone would meet me at the airport at 2 a.m. to escort me to this flat they had graciously found.

Ricky picked me up as promised and delivered me safely to the flat. The family that offered me accommodation also arranged tickets to the Taj Mahal, and I would have to take the second-class train to Agra the following day as the first-class seats were all sold out.

Naively, I set out in my western clothes the next day (walking shorts and a short-sleeve t-shirt). It took no time at all to be reminded I was a Calgary girl on a new frontier. I received hard looks of disapproval from everyone on my journey and was told I should keep my head and eyes cast politely downward and not make eye contact. I adhered to this advice and tried my best to resist the growing discomfort.

This was an excellent learning experience about how crucial it is to do your research and due diligence before you travel anywhere outside your home territory. The reasons are numerous: safety and security, to honour and respect local culture and decorum, to blend in easier and thus better enjoy the experience.

Back at the flat later, I shared my experience with the flat 'mom.' She prudently recommended I don a sari for my future ventures away from the flat. After that, it was a breeze to move to and from the many locations, meetings and sights I experienced while in India. My childlike curiosity was fulfilled. I met incredible success at the trade show. My wardrobe caused quite a stir as I manned the Alberta booth and also promoted our career handbook. Indian citizens and other foreigners lined up to learn more about the Western woman wearing a sari. It was easy to fall in love with such a dynamic and warm country and its people. I made many connections that I still nurture today. Now I never leave home without researching my destination and I always keep "When in Rome ..." as my motto.

CAT'S CHALLENGE

We believe what is meant for you is on it's way. Saying "yes" to the universe and what you are invited to participate in, is part of the process of attracting the job of your dreams.

At the end of every seminar, Catherine challenges the participants with the following:

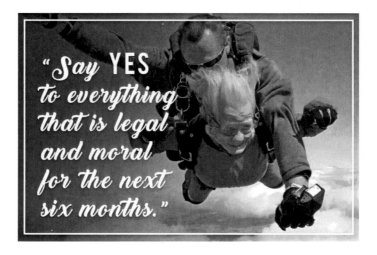

ACKNOWLEDGMENTS

DEDICATION:

Catherine would like to dedicate this book to her father, Robert Brownlee (1938 – 2017), who always believed in her and supported her dreams. Robert had many wonderful "dadisms," such as:

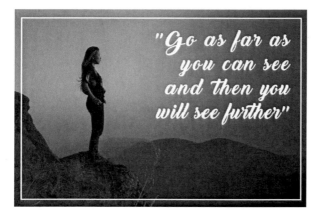

"Go as far as you can see and then you will see further"

And another favourite:

"When you see a turtle on top of a fencepost, you know he didn't get there all by himself."

Nobody gets anywhere without everyone. With that in mind, we want to acknowledge and thank all those who helped in the creation of this book.

CONTRIBUTORS

Stan Peake, exceptional Business Coach and Mentor
InSite Performance Coaching Ltd.

> Email: stan@insiteperformancecoaching.com
>
> Website: www.insiteperformancecoaching.com

Carmen Goss, the best ever Career Coach

> Email: carmen@carmengoss.com

Heather Morin, New Dimension Design

> Email: heather@nddesign.ca
>
> Website: nddesign.ca

Eric Termuende, Speaker, Author, Entrepreneur

> Website: www.erictermuende.com
>
> www.nsb.com/speakers/eric-termuende/

Thomas Labelle, Certified Career Development Professional /Coach

> Email: coachthom@me.com

DESIGN:

Monika Collins, Graphic Designer

> Email: hello@monikacollins.com
>
> Portfolio: www.monikacollins.com

Natalie Robertson

> LinkedIn: www.linkedin.com/in/nataliejrobertson/

EDITING:

Lyn Cadence, Cadence PR

Email: lyn@cadencepr.ca

Website: cadencepr.ca

Kathy Dueck

Email: kay.dueck@gmail.com

Website: ksdueck.com

LinkedIn: www.linkedin.com/in/thewritingninja/

Facebook: @theWritingNinja

Carrie Gour

Email: carrie@writeongirl.com

INSPIRED BY:

Heather Johnson, co-author of our bestseller in 2007, *Want to Work in Oil and Gas?*

ABOUT THE AUTHORS

CATHERINE BROWNLEE

Catherine Brownlee is the President and CEO of CBI, where she brings over 30 years' experience in executive search, business development, marketing strategies and networking around the globe. In 2017 her database was over 85,000 contacts, which demonstrates her capacity to motivate, build and achieve results. Catherine's passion is to serve and support the obsession of the world's most courageous change agents by removing barriers and opening doors. She was recognized by her peers as one of the celebrated Women of Influence in Calgary and was a Paul Harris Award recipient through the Rotary Club of Calgary.

Catherine is a recognized expert and speaker on the subject of industry strategies and advancements. She developed and regularly presents the popular seminar, "How to get the job of your dreams." She co-authored the best-selling book *Want to Work in Oil and Gas?*

Cat's Tips to Get the Job of Your Dreams provides strategies for getting the job of your dreams – anywhere in the world.

In her spare time, Catherine is committed to serving her community as Co-Chairman of the Rotary Tom Jackson Stay in School initiative and member of the Rotary Club of Calgary. Her passion is seen in the areas of human rights, serving children and our vulnerable population.

LIANE ANGERMAN

Liane Angerman obtained her Bachelor of Arts degree with a major in English from Mount Royal University in Calgary (2007). Her passion for communications has landed her on the boards of directors for several energy startup corporations. She has a myriad of publishing credits ranging from fiction, lifestyle, health, technical, fashion, legal, corporate and educational.

She performed as associate editor and features writer for the OGM, a global energy magazine, and as Publisher, Western Canada for a luxury publication from Montreal, as well as a local Montreal-based magazine.

While living in Connecticut and studying at the Institute of Children's Literature, she wrote her first young adult novel. *Season of Haze* was published in Pittsburgh in 2006. Currently, she is crafting an erotic thriller and living in Western Canada.

KAREN COTTINGHAM

Karen Cottingham has called Calgary home since 1983. Largely self-taught, she spent many years in the corporate world, where her position in customer service led to a penchant for organization and process improvement.

After corporate layoffs in the 1990s, Karen discovered her entrepreneurial spirit, her refusal to accept defeat and her love of writing. From 1995 to 2007, she was editor, graphic designer and publisher of *Our World 50+*, a lifestyle magazine for the baby boomer generation. She now provides virtual business services to select clients, who have come to appreciate her savvy, competence and timely results.

Now semi-retired, she divides her time between her client base, gardening/landscaping and her four delightful grandchildren.

Cat's Tips to Get the Job of Your Dreams brings over 30 years' experience in career placement and the search industry. Drawing on the experiences and inspirational stories of hundreds of candidates, this book offers tried and true wisdom with practical recommendations. By following these tips, tools and tales, you will learn how to be in the right place at the right time, and then know what to do and say when you get there. These career search methods have proven results and, when followed, they will work for you too!

"As a business leader, I know there is nothing more important than getting the right people on our teams to do the work that our stakeholders expect of us. *Cat's Tips* will bring outstanding candidates to organizations around the world."

~ Steve Allan,
Chair of Calgary Economic Development
Recipient of the Order of Canada and the Alberta Order of Excellence

"I have seen firsthand the positive influence of Catherine Brownlee's work. Her guidance has made a big difference in the lives of people looking for a new career or expanding their personal networks. I am excited she and her co-authors are now sharing their knowledge and expertise with a global audience."

~ Greg Clark,
MLA for Calgary Elbow

"*Cat's Tips to Get the Job of Your Dreams* gives job-seekers a distinct advantage over their competitors in today's marketplace. With loads of information packed into one easy-to-navigate book, *Cat's Tips* shows you how to write your own success stories, map the career of your dreams and get connected. This book is a timely contribution as we position and re-position ourselves in a shifting economy."

~ Lyn Cadence,
PR Strategist, Publicist & Coach, Cadence PR

"Catherine and her team have put together an insightful, actionable guide to landing a job in a world that is evolving faster than it ever has before. This book is a quick read that will surely give you the insights and tools required to not just land any job, but the right job for you. A must-read for those looking to get (and stay) ahead in their job searching efforts."

~ Eric Termuende,
Co-founder NoW Innovations, Author of *Rethink Work*